HOW TO
STAY ALIVE
AS LONG AS
YOU LIVE

HOW TO STAY ALIVE

AS LONG AS YOU LIVE

Practical Guides
for Christian Living

ROBERT H. SPAIN

DIMENSIONS
FOR LIVING

NASHVILLE

HOW TO STAY ALIVE AS LONG AS YOU LIVE

Copyright © 1992 by Dimensions for Living

This book is printed on recycled, acid-free paper.

Library of Congress Cataloging-in-Publication Data

Spain, Robert H., 1925–
  How to stay alive as long as you live : practical guides for
Christian living / Robert H. Spain.
      p.   cm.
  ISBN 0-687-17942-4 (alk. paper)
  1. Christian life—1960–   I. Title.
BV4501.2.S67   1992
248.4—dc20   92-323
                                                                                CIP

MANUFACTURED IN THE UNITED STATES OF AMERICA

To my wife, Syble,
a faithful companion in ministry

CONTENTS

HOW TO
STAY ALIVE
AS LONG AS
YOU LIVE

I

HOW TO STAY ALIVE AS LONG AS YOU LIVE

A familiar joke goes this way. Some ministers were discussing the issue of when life begins. "Life begins," said the Catholic priest, "at the moment of conception." "No, no, Father," said the Presbyterian minister. "Life begins at the moment of birth." Both of them turned to the aging Jewish rabbi. "Life begins," said the rabbi, slowly stroking his beard, "when the kids leave home and the dog dies."

This chapter is not about the beginning of life. It is about *staying* alive as long as you live. It is often said that life begins at forty. I am not going to argue that point. Another generally held belief is life is over when one reaches retirement. That doesn't leave many years in between. Life, *real* life, can begin whenever you want it to begin, and it can go on and on and on—regardless of age. It is not living but *staying alive as long as you live* that is important!

Accept Yourself as a Person of Worth.

Our value is often measured by what we can do, how much we can produce or control. Worth is evaluated too often by our accomplishments.

11

In his book *Hide or Seek,* James Dobson tells of John McKay, football coach at the University of Southern California. McKay's son, John, was a successful player on his dad's team. When asked to comment on the pride he felt for his son's accomplishments on the field, McKay answered: "Yes, I'm pleased that John had a good season last year. He does a fine job and I am proud of him. But I would be just as proud if he had never played the game at all."

McKay teaches us a good lesson. John's football talent is recognized and appreciated, but his human worth does not depend on his ability to play football. Worth is more than accomplishment or position.

Ida Eisenhower, mother of President Dwight D. Eisenhower, was asked in an interview if she was proud of her son. She answered, "Yes, I am very proud. Which son?"

You came into this world filled with worth. One of the most tragic diseases is the inability to accept your worth. It is a crippling sickness, and it afflicts persons of all ages. There are two symptoms of this emotional virus.

The first symptom is the depression that comes from not being able to do some of the things you once could do. You may not verbalize this depression, but you think about earlier days when you could do things that are now impossible. Rationally, you know this is the way it is with life, but it is hard to accept.

I was in the gym one day watching a group of young boys playing basketball. As a young person, I played a fairly good game. My ability to jump was pretty good. As I talked with the boys, I said something about how I used to dunk the ball. Later, during a break in the action, one of the boys said, "Let's see you dunk it," and he tossed the ball in my direction. Naturally, I was eager to show my ability, and I took the ball and headed for the goal. About halfway up, I made a startling discovery. There was no way! My legs couldn't do it. Sure, I used to do it, but that day has passed. There are other things I can't do today that I once could do. That's all right. I'm not twenty-five anymore. I'm not fifty anymore. The sooner I recognize this, the better I will be. But my physical limitations have nothing to do with my worth as a person.

In some buildings the clocks are connected to a central control system so that they automatically reset themselves every day at a predetermined time. For us, resetting our clocks is not a possibility. Our clocks keep ticking. Part of staying alive is accepting ourselves as we are, concentrating on what we can do, and trying not to duplicate our past.

It is helpful to remember that you can do some things now that you could not do earlier in life. The waning of some skills opens the door for new ones. Besides, there are some things that you do not need to do or want to do now.

The second symptom of this disease is a longing to be like someone else. This is a tough one. Early in my ministry I wanted to be like the great preachers I heard. I woke up one day to the fact that I was not one of them; and if I were going to be anything, I should start being me. I still wish for many abilities and skills I see in others, but I have learned to accept myself for what I am. This does not mean that I am satisfied with what I am, but God has given me a body and a mind and has challenged me to use them in the best way possible.

You can't replay the tape and retrace your life of yesterday. You can't be someone else. That's all right. Your worth has not changed. Accept yourself and celebrate what you have. It will keep you alive as long as you live.

Nurture Your Reason for Being.

A purpose, a goal, a dream—these are the ingredients for staying alive. You are a person of worth; there is a reason for your being.

Centuries ago, God said to Joshua that the promised land would belong to him and his people, but they would have to arise and go possess it. That is what God is saying to us. I have a plan for your life. I have a dream for this world, and you are a part of that dream.

The nearest thing to death is when there is no meaningful purpose for which to live. Purpose, not wealth or success, makes life worthwhile. Life is tragic for the person who has plenty to live on but nothing to live for. In *The Courage to Create*, Rollo May suggests that a person with no purpose is a contradiction in terms.

Viktor Frankl left his mark upon the world as one of this century's greatest psychiatrists. At his death, he was the leading professor of psychiatry and neurology at the University of Vienna. In his book *Man's Search for Meaning* he described his experiences in the Auschwitz concentration camp in Germany. He wrote that anyone who has a *why* to live can endure almost any *how*. According to Frankl, the people who survived that terrible ordeal had something that gave their survival meaning. Those who had nothing to live for succumbed to the horrors of the camp.

Thomas Huxley said we can sustain no greater shock than the sense of uselessness. This sense of uselessness affects persons of all ages. It has been estimated that about 25 percent of all people can be compared to a ship without a rudder. Whatever you do, you must keep your dreams alive. If you have no dreams, you can have no dreams come true. We may not be able to do all we want to do, but that should not keep us from doing the things we can do.

George Washington Carver had a big dream. According to Carver, he cried out to God to let him do something big in the world. God said, "No, the world is too big for you to do something about, but here's a peanut. Let's see what you can do with it." That is exactly what he did.

A reason for being has nothing to do with age. In the later years of life, some may welcome a change of pace, but usefulness and age are not related. The mature years may be the most useful and meaningful of all; they may provide the opportunity to pursue dreams and goals without the interruptions and responsibilities experienced in earlier years. This may be the time for which you have been waiting.

A reason for being, a purpose, is important for life at any age. Nurture your purpose every day. It will keep you alive as long as you live.

Develop a Positive Mental Attitude.

In the past fifty years, more has been written on this subject than in any other period of history. Unraveling the mysteries of the mind ranks at the top of the list of accomplishments. In her book *What Are You?* Imelda Shanklin said that we use our thoughts as tools to carve our life stories on the substance of the universe. By ruling our minds, we rule our worlds. By choosing our thoughts, we choose our outcomes. In other words, our lives are what we think.

One of my concerns about today's movies, TV shows, books, and magazines is that, over the years, we will become like our mental handling of these things. Our minds feed on these thoughts as a computer receives information. What is put in eventually comes out. Our thinking shapes our behavior and determines our attitudes.

In the fifties the acronym PMA—Positive Mental Attitude—became popular. Every major seminar leader built a lecture around it. Norman Vincent Peale brought it to the forefront of religious groups. Today Robert Schuller of the Crystal Cathedral is sounding the message. Our minds are the rudders of our ships. The impulses of our brains determine the persons we become.

Norman Cousins spent most of his life as editor of *Saturday Review*. In the latter years of his life, he worked with the medical school at UCLA to help patients use their mental powers for healing. He knew that people could make themselves ill, and he discovered that people also could improve their health. There was ample evidence to show that positive emotions could affect biological responses to illness. He concluded that the mind, working through the body, can produce an immune system to meet the challenge of illness.

Some have a difficult time developing positive mental attitudes. Nothing is ever right for them. The world is bad. They see nothing good anywhere. They are like the old farmer who was always complaining about the insects or the weather or the low price at the market. Finally, a year came when all the conditions were favorable and he brought in a bumper crop. "Well, you have it made now," said a friend. "Yeah, it's fair," answered the farmer, "but a harvest like this is pretty hard on the soil." For some, nothing is ever right.

Our attitude is the mirror of our minds. We are the reflection of our thoughts. While much of the study of the mind is a new science, long ago Paul wrote to the church at Philippi: "Whatever is true, whatever is honorable, whatever is just, whatever is pure, whatever is pleasing, whatever is commendable, if there is any excellence and if there is anything worthy of praise, think about these things" (Philippians 4:8). Paul also wrote, "Be transformed by the renewing of your minds" (Romans 12:2).

A positive mind is a key to staying alive as long as you live.

Give Your Life Away.

We know the scripture, "It is more blessed to give than to receive" (Acts 20:35*b*). This is absolutely true. It often has been said that we help ourselves when we sincerely try to help another. To get, you have to give.

One of the best sermons of all time was written with a stub of a pencil on two sides of a sheet of wrapping paper and placed for protection in a baking powder can. The can was wired to an old pump, the only source of water along a lonely trail in the western desert. This is what was written:

This pump is all right as of June, 1932. I put a new sucker washer into it and it ought to last five years. But the washer dries out and the pump has got to be primed. Under the white rock I buried a bottle of water out of the sun and cork end up. There's enough water in it to prime the pump—but not if you drink some first. Pour about ¼ and let her soak to wet the leather. Then pour in the rest medium fast and pump like heck. You'll git water. The well has never run dry. Have faith. When you git watered up, fill the bottle and put it back like you found it for the next feller. (Signed) Desert Pete.

P.S. Don't go drinkin' up the water first. Prime the pump with it and you'll git all you can hold. And next time you want something remember that life is like this pump. It has to be primed. I've give my last dime away a dozen times to prime my pump—and I've fed my last bean to a stranger. It never failed yet to git me an answer. You got to git your heart fixed to give before you can be give to.

Helen Keller once said she would do more than spend her life; she would *invest* it. That is what Albert Schweitzer did in Africa and what Mother Teresa is doing in India. Those who soak up all that is around them and keep it to themselves cannot truly live. Life comes as we give it away.

Some time ago, I gave the keynote address at a national stewardship conference. I was assigned the topic "Good News About Giving." The chief consideration was financial giving, but I also talked about the giving of human resources—the giving of ourselves. Sharing ourselves is a major means of God's grace. The scriptures are clear: Life comes only as we give it away. These words from Malachi are true: God will pour "down for you an overflowing blessing" (3:10*b*). That doesn't necessarily mean that God will give us material things but that God will give us life. The surest way to emotional death is to be on the receiving end of everything.

For grace to abound, our giving should be sacrificial. A friend of mine used to say to me, "Spain, you never give anything until you have to do without something you need to make the gift possible." A hymn expresses it well:

> Love so amazing, so divine,
> Demands my life, my soul, my all.

We also should be a little reckless in our giving. Once when Jesus was in Bethany, a woman rushed into the house, broke an alabaster jar, and poured all the contents on him. That wasn't planned. That was a burst of emotion born out of love. It was extravagant recklessness.

There is a story about a college president who had an old wooden turtle on his desk. It didn't seem to belong in a well-furnished office. Everyone who came to see him asked about it. He would hold it up for them to read the inscription on the bottom. It said: "Remember the turtle. He only makes progress when he sticks his neck out."

I see recklessness in other areas of life. Have you ever gotten "caught up" in an auction? Your spirit gets carried away, and you bid beyond what you had planned. It would be good if we could put a little bit of this recklessness into the sharing of ourselves.

What are you doing for others? Some have found their spirits soaring by babysitting a young couple's children. Some are volunteers at the hospital or some social agency. Some keep the nursery at the church or teach Sunday school or tutor underprivileged children. Some sew for the Red Cross or read to the blind. Others go regularly to nursing homes. I know one person who has found meaning in his life by driving persons in need to the doctor. Where you give yourself will depend upon your personal skills and abilities, your physical condition, the availability of transportation, and family demands. The act doesn't have to be big. A part of life is doing something for others. That "something" is more than a good gesture; it is inherent in the way God made us. Life comes as we give it away. Giving your life away is a part of staying alive as long as you live.

Remember That God Is with You.

There is a story about a young Native American boy who had to undergo the customary ritual before assuming manhood. He had to prove to the community that he was brave and could withstand the troubles of the world. To do this, he had to go out into the forest and spend a night alone. He could take nothing with him except a knife for protection. All night long he had to listen to the strange sounds and wait for whatever would come. It was only later that the young boy learned that his father had been standing nearby all night, watching over him.

This is the way it is with us. God is always nearby, watching. We can count on it. His love and presence are with us forever—whatever we do.

In one of my former churches there was a woman who had a house filled with antiques. She was an interesting person who didn't mince words with anyone. You didn't always agree with her, but you always knew where you stood and where she stood. She seemed to like me and invited me to come to her house and pick out one of her antiques. She would not give it to me immediately but would leave it to me in her will.

I looked the antiques over and chose an old brass oil-fed student lamp. It was a beautiful piece—dark green shade with the old brass oil container still in perfect condition. She told me I had made a good choice.

She then took out a piece of masking tape from her desk and wrote my name on it and put it on the bottom of the lamp. Then she asked me to notice how easily the tape went on and how easily it came off. She said, "Now, as long as you suit me, I'll leave your name on this lamp. When you don't, I'll take it off."

God's love is not like this. It grieves God's heart when we behave in ways contrary to his will, but he never forsakes us. God is like the Native American father standing watch over us, protecting and caring for us despite what we do.

An elderly person said to me one day, "There is not a soul in this world who cares whether I live or die." I doubt that was the case at all. Even so, there is one who is of the world and beyond the world who does care. We can rest in the assurance that we are never alone. God is always near. That knowledge will keep you alive as long as you live.

God sent his Son into the world so that we might live abundantly—not just later, but *now*. Jesus came to empower us for a meaningful life. With Jesus at your side, it is amazing what the two of you can do.

There is a story about Paderewski, one of the world's leading pianists. At one of Paderewski's concerts, the crowd anxiously awaited his arrival. A nine-year-old boy grew impatient with all the waiting but was fascinated with the beautiful Steinway piano on the stage. The boy slipped away from his parents to explore the beautiful instrument. Oblivious to the crowd in the concert hall, he sat down at the piano and began to play his favorite rendition of "Chopsticks."

The crowd was stunned. Some laughed, others cried out in anger, and some yelled for the ushers to take him out. Backstage, Paderewski looked out to see about the noise and saw the young lad sitting where he was soon to be. He quickly went out, took his seat beside the young boy, and began playing a beautiful counterharmony. The boy was confused by the presence of another, so Paderewski told him quietly to keep playing. He assured the boy that he was doing great and that they could do it together.

That is what Jesus Christ does for us. He came to be with us; and, though the music of our lives may be incomplete, he will help to make something beautiful out of it. With Christ at your side, you can stay alive as long as you live.

* * *

You can stay alive—really *alive*—as long as you live if you . . .

- Accept yourself as a person of worth.
- Nurture your reason for being.
- Develop a positive mental attitude.
- Give your life away.
- Remember that God is with you.

It's great to be alive!

II

HOW TO PUT FIRST THINGS FIRST

Setting priorities is tough business. Acting on them is even tougher. Decision making is a constant demand of life, and, for many, it is a frustrating experience.

A child is presented a bowl of assorted candies and is told to choose one of them. Which one? The red one—or the green one—or would the striped one be better—or maybe the one wrapped in golden foil? Children are usually delighted to have such an offer, but sometimes the frustration of making the choice almost overcomes the joy.

A teenage boy is playing Monopoly and lands on a space that can be purchased. He considers the opportunity, counts his money, looks at the space, and again looks at his money. Someone yells, "Come on, do something!" How does he decide which is the better move? It's tough.

In bigger and more important circles it is the same. The federal government is trying to build a budget for the coming year. There are programs galore that would do wonders for the people, but there is a limited amount of money. As in the Monopoly game, a decision has to be made. The church faces such decisions every year when the opportunities for ministry exceed the anticipated income. Decision making is also a regular dilemma in most family circles. What decisions are best? Making choices and setting priorities are tough business.

It is no different in your life. Here, however, the stakes are even higher. The child may fret over the choice of candy, but any piece probably will be all right. The young boy may sweat a bit over the Monopoly opportunity, but it is only a game. Choices and decisions about your life are different. Life is not a game; life is for real. What career path will you follow? What business will you buy? Where will you move your family? How will you use your human resources for the best results? How will you determine the direction of your life? What will be the primary focus of your life?

Jesus told a parable about a merchant whose primary focus was finding the greatest of all pearls: "The kingdom of heaven is like a merchant in search of fine pearls; on finding one pearl of great value, he went and sold all that he had and bought it" (Matthew 13:45-46). This story about choosing the most important thing in life has been repeated time and time again. It has been the subject of countless sermons admonishing people to disregard the secondary things and go after those things that are really important. The message is sound; that is what we should do. But how did this merchant make that decision? What were the measures he used to come to that conclusion?

There is a beautiful and moving story in Nehemiah about the rebuilding of the walls of Jerusalem. It is an exciting testimony of the people's willingness to do what was needed. As you may recall, they were faced with several alternatives, but they did not give in to any of them. The rebuilding of the wall was their priority, and that is what they did. But the question remains: How did they reach that decision?

You've often heard that you should "put first things first," but how do you know what is first? What are the rules for this exercise? How do you make such decisions?

Come to Grips with Who You Are.

A decade or so ago it seemed that every workshop or seminar I attended began with this question: Who are you? Frankly, I grew weary of it. But the truth is that if you have not answered this question for yourself, you have no basis for making decisions about your life. "First things" will depend upon who you think you are. Who are you?

You are a created being—not the creator. In Paul's letter to the Ephesians, he tells us that God had us in mind before the world was founded. He designed us and arranged for our adoption through Jesus Christ. This means that as a created being, you are not in control of everything. The world does not run by your personal clock. The whole universe is not in your hands. The world existed before you arrived on the scene, and the world will exist after you are gone. You are not self-made. You did not create yourself; you were created.

As a created being, you are endowed with gifts and abilities. You came into this world with a pantry filled with ingredients. You have a supply room that is chocked full of useful commodities. These commodities are not the same for everyone, but they all have worth. You did not earn these gifts, nor buy them. They were gifts. You may envy the gifts of others, but that doesn't give you those gifts. You have been given your own supply, and that is what you have to work with. These gifts and abilities are the seeds from which beautiful things can be grown; they are the ingredients from which delicious treats can be made. Your gifts represent possibilities. You can use your abilities to be either a contributing or destructive force in life. It's up to you.

You also are the product of others, but you are not controlled by them. There are others in the world who, like you, also were created. They have impacted your life, and your personal lockbox is filled with their contributions. You are one of many. You are part of a world family. The others who share this planet with you have made and are making a contribution to your life. You have a responsibility to them, but your life is not controlled by them. You are free to pursue your own life.

Come to Grips with Whose You Are.

You are a creature of God—made in God's image. You have the stamp of God's Spirit etched on your soul. Just as kings of long ago cast their own images upon coins to remind everyone whose coins they were, so also God has put a mark upon you. Some have described this phenomenon by saying God is like a big ball of fire and a spark from that fire is implanted within each of us. The relationship you have with the Creator is so powerful that the spark within you is seeking constantly to reestablish itself with its source. Knowingly or unknowingly, God is in you and is struggling to find expression through you. Inside you is a homing spirit that tugs you toward God.

A woman who was hearing about God for the first time sat quietly as the missionary spoke softly and clearly. The more she heard, the more captivated she became. Finally, she could contain herself no longer. She leapt to her feet and cried, "I knew it! I knew it! I knew there had to be such a one. I have felt it inside me all my life."

God has not only put his mark upon you, but God also has made you special. You are a unique creation. The print of your finger or thumb is unlike all the others God has made. The pitch and tone of your voice are so different from all others that electronic devices can distinguish your voice from others. Your DNA is different from anyone else's. You are not the only creation of God, but you are distinctive. You are unique.

Jesus came to bridge the gap that separated us from God. He came to unite the created with the Creator. Without this relationship, we cannot live up to our potential or fulfill our purpose as human beings. Apart from life in relationship with

God, our existence centers basically upon ourselves. That leads to a narrow focus which corrupts life rather than enhances it.

The *whose* you are says much about your priorities. You are free, but you are not your own. Your relationship with God speaks volumes about the decisions you make in life.

Come to Grips with Why You Are.

The basketball player knows why she races down the court with the ball. (It is not so she can show off her dribbling skills or impress the crowd with her speed.) The baseball player knows why he is up to bat. The salesperson knows why she is calling on customers. The doctor knows why he is prescribing a particular medication. What is the "why" of your life? Until you know the "why," you cannot make right decisions.

Why do you think God created this world of people? Why do you think God created you? An old catechism teaches us that our "why" is to glorify God and to live for God forever. It is God's plan to have a family that works cooperatively with God to build a world where righteousness and goodness are the foundation of a just and lasting society. God is the power, and we are the hands and feet and eyes and ears. We are the instruments through which God expresses and uses the power for the benefit of the world. The fulfillment of God's plan is our reason for being. We can live outside that plan and go our own way, but that is not God's hope for us. We are to use our lives so that God's desire for the world becomes a reality.

Using your life to fulfill God's will does not mean that you must be a preacher or missionary. The purposes of God must be expressed in all areas of life. Within any honorable work are vast opportunities for helping to build a better world. The school teacher does it by teaching and building relationships. Mothers and fathers do it by nurturing children. The engineer does it by designing and maintaining safe and productive equipment. The farmer does it by growing healthy foods and practicing good stewardship of the land. Everyone has a "why." Only when you know "why" can you know the priorities of life.

The *who* you are defines the possibilities. The *whose* you are provides the power. The *why* you are determines the need and sounds the marching orders. Most of the complications in decision making stem from not having an answer to these basics of life. Remember that *being* always precedes *doing*. The *who*, *whose*, and *why* are the prelude to decision making. After answering these questions for yourself, you are then ready to move to the *doing* stage—to put first things first.

Take a Realistic Inventory of Your Personal Pantry.

In business there is a time for taking an inventory of the merchandise. Estimates are not good enough. There must be an accounting of everything in stock. Only then will there be sufficient information for future ordering. It is no different in your life. You have been given a well-stocked pantry, but it is important to know as much as possible about what is in that pantry. Everyone has meaningful possibilities, but no one can do everything. It is here that we begin to separate desire from fact.

I love music. I have a tremendous desire to be a participant, in some way, in music. I hear those deep baritone voices and I want to sing like them, but I can't. I confess that I envy those who can sing, but I know that my pantry doesn't include some of the necessary ingredients.

I also wish I had a voice like some of the speakers I've heard. As a young preacher, I tried occasionally to speak like them, but it didn't work. I discovered that I had to work with what I had. That was not negative. It simply meant that I had to find my own place and use those gifts that had been given to me.

Do you know the dimensions of *your* possibilities? Have you made a realistic appraisal of your personal abilities? There are those who piously proclaim in loud voices that you can do anything you want to do. I appreciate their positive motivational efforts, but it is better for you to look at your inventory list. If you want to build a house, then you must see whether you have wood or brick or stone in your warehouse. A good house can be built with any of these materials. Your decision is determined by your personal materials.

The disciples began this realistic inventory of their lives when they met with Jesus in the Upper Room. They may have had great dreams about their lives, but by asking "Is it I?" they began the process of seeing themselves as they were.

When making right decisions—putting first things first—the beginning is understanding yourself. Your given ingredients determine your possibilities. Please remember, however, that many of your ingredients are seeds that can be planted and nurtured. All your possibilities have not come to you full-grown. Your first task is to determine the contents of your pantry.

Chip Away All Self-fulfilling Desires.

There is a story about a man who had a huge boulder in his front yard. He grew weary of this big stone being the centerpiece of his lawn, so he decided to turn it into a work of art. He chipped away at the stone until it became a beautiful stone elephant. A neighbor asked, "How did you ever carve such a marvelous likeness of an elephant?" He answered that he simply chipped away everything that didn't look like an elephant. Likewise, Michelangelo said that as he worked with stone he released the form that was within it. He chipped away everything that didn't resemble the form he had in mind.

You have been made in the image of God, and you must chip away everything that doesn't fit the person God wants you to be. This relationship with your Creator gives direction to the

27

decisions you make about your life. To be all we are capable of being may require the chipping away of selfish ambition or envy or excessive pride or uncontrollable anger. It will be different for each of us. Whatever hinders you from being all you are capable of being must go. Your life, and the decisions you face, must be ordered by this unique and beautiful relationship you have with God.

Years ago Copernicus and Galileo made some remarkable discoveries about our solar system. Until their time, the earth was thought to be the center of the solar system. From their studies they concluded that the sun, not the earth, was the center. If the sun were not the center, they reasoned, then the movements of the solar system would make no sense. There would be no meaning or purpose in all the movements of the sky.

What Copernicus and Galileo discovered about the solar system, Jesus discovered and taught about life. *We* are not center stage. We sometimes act as if we were, but we are not. If we see ourselves as the center, then life is robbed of its meaning and purpose. God is the center of our lives, and everything that does not relate us to that center must be chipped away. When we do this, we discover the beautiful form that is unleashed.

Set Your Internal Compass Toward the Purpose of Your Being.

The spark of fire within you becomes your internal compass, pointing and pulling you toward the purposes of God.

My car has a built-in compass. Soon after getting the car, I noticed that the compass was flawed—or so I thought. When I traveled what I knew to be south, it pointed east. I couldn't rely on it. I searched the car's manual for an answer and discovered that the compass had to be set. I was to point the car to the north and set the compass on north. When I did that, the compass worked correctly.

Your internal compass gives you direction for your life. It gives you a purpose. It answers the "why" of your being. It provides a focus for your decisions.

Have you ever held a magnifying glass on a bright sunny day so that it captures the sun's rays? Through the glass you can focus the sun's broad rays on a pinpoint, causing extreme heat capable of setting fire to a piece of paper. That is what God can do with your life. He can take away the fragmentation and bring unity and pinpoint purpose.

Thomas Carlyle once wrote that, without a purpose, we are like a ship without a rudder. That is absolutely true, but any purpose will not do. This is why the compass is important. It points you in the direction of a meaningful purpose, and this gives value to all that you do. For the person on a prison chain gang cutting stones from a quarry, the work is a never-ending, monotonous routine. For the sculptor, however, cutting the stone is an exciting adventure. The difference is purpose. Life has to have purpose to be meaningful. Without it, your ship is without a rudder, wandering around without direction.

There is a reason for your being. When that reason or focus becomes clear, you are on your way to putting first things first.

* * *

The possibilities for your life are determined by the discovery of *who* you are. The power you need to fulfill these possibilities is given when you realize *whose* you are. The purpose for your life is determined by *why* you are. Once you have come to grips with *who, whose,* and *why* you are . . .

- Take a realistic inventory of your personal pantry.
- Chip away all self-fulfilling desires.
- Set your internal compass toward the purpose of your being.

This will give a focus to your life that will wash away indecision and mixed signals. You will be free to put first things first!

III

HOW TO HANDLE DETOURS

Most of us are allergic to detours. The sign suddenly appears, and a peculiar sensation begins to settle over us. Our route has been carefully planned. Others are waiting for us, and we're exactly on time—then the DETOUR sign appears. It may be that a bridge is being repaired or the road is being rebuilt—it doesn't matter. The fact remains that our planned journey has been interrupted.

Detours also confront us as we travel through life. Our goals are set. Our schedule is in place. Everything is "go," and suddenly it hits. Illness comes when we can least afford it. The company closes its doors when our need for work is greatest. War is declared, and we are called to serve our country at the exact moment our careers are beginning to blossom. Even in little matters *it* happens. The water stops at the very moment we are lathered up with soap. The football is on the one-yard line, it's the fourth down—then the phone rings. You never have had a flat tire until you are on your way to a job interview. Murphy's law sometimes seems to be the controlling force of life: If anything can go wrong, it will.

Detours are a normal part of life. In the movie *Oh God, Book Two,* George Burns, playing the part of God, is asked by a little girl why bad things happen. Burns thinks about her question and then says that the system simply works that way. He asks her if she has ever seen an up without a down, a front without a back, or a top without a bottom. He then explains that you can't have one without the other. In one of the delightful Uncle Remus tales, wise old Brer Fox tells Brer Rabbit that you can't run away from trouble—there "ain't no place" that far. The road of life is filled with detours. Interruptions are everywhere. Burns was right: That's the way the system works.

Acknowledge That Some of Life's Detours Are of Your Own Making.

We bring some detours upon ourselves. We are traveling at a high rate of speed, can't make the turn, and plow into an embankment or a rock wall. That is an interruption of our own making. Occasionally we read of one who takes a shortcut to financial security. Through burglary or embezzlement, the detour appears. We have been saddened by the difficulty experienced by one of baseball's greatest players, Pete Rose, but he brought it upon himself. Wagering on baseball games is against the rules. He broke that rule, so he has no one to blame but himself. Some students may have their minds set on a particular career, but their hearts are leading to more fun and less study; their career goals are washed away. These are detours of their own making.

Accept That Some of Life's Detours Are Not of Your Own Making.

Some detours are thrust upon us by outside forces. A family member has an illness. The company where we have worked for twenty years closes its doors. Our eyesight begins to fade. Our

31

mind is not as sharp as it once was. The business burns to the ground.

John James Audubon is noted for his drawings and paintings of birds. He wandered all over North America for ten years with his brush and pen and crayons, sketching over one thousand birds. He took this ten years' worth of work to a friend in Philadelphia and left the collection until he could arrange for publication. When he returned to pick up his works, he discovered that rats had gotten into the boxes and destroyed every drawing. That's an interruption from an outside force.

Some interruptions are of your own doing and some of them come upon you from the outside, but you can count on this: Detours will come, and in some way you must handle them.

The big question remains: *How?* Before trying to answer, let me suggest two things you must not do.

Never View a Detour as the End of the Road.

Detours are sometimes short, occasionally long; but if you persevere, you will get back on course. The fact that these unexpected obstacles do come doesn't mean that life is over.

An unlettered maid was great in the kitchen and was an immaculate housekeeper, but her main strength was that she was never ruffled by anything. She was always calm and in control. When asked about her secret, she quoted a verse in the Bible: "It came to pass." When told this was not the complete verse, she replied, "It is for me. It means that whatever comes, comes to pass. It doesn't come to stay."

For many, detours have not been the end of the road. Einstein could not speak until he was four years old and did not begin to read until he was seven. Beethoven's music teacher said that Beethoven was hopeless as a composer. When Thomas Edison was a young boy, his teachers said he was so stupid he could never learn anything. F. W. Woolworth got a job in a store at age twenty-one, but he was not allowed to serve any customers because he didn't have "enough sense." Walt Disney was once fired by a newspaper editor because he didn't have any good ideas. Caruso was told by his music teacher that he had no voice at all.

I am fascinated by the work of glass blowers. Good blowers may work all day without a mistake. When flaws occasionally do appear, they do not throw the work away but begin with the error and transform it into another design. The same thing is true with those who weave oriental carpets. When an error comes, they weave it into another pattern. Potters, too, continue to work with the clay even when it doesn't yield the design they have in mind.

In life, flaws, obstacles, difficulties, and detours come, but they do not mark the end of the road.

Don't Wallow in Self-pity.

In the first place, wallowing in self-pity doesn't impress anyone else; and second, it eats away at you until it robs you of whatever you have left. Everyone has had some kind of trouble. You are not the only one who has stumbled or found life hard.

There is a story of a man who went through the great flood of the Ohio Valley in the 1930s. It was a tragic experience, but he couldn't get over it. He talked about his unfortunate experience constantly. When he died and went to heaven, Saint Peter asked him if there were anything he would especially like to do. The man said he would like Saint Peter to get a crowd together so that he could tell them of his horrible experience in the Ohio Valley flood. Saint Peter called together a crowd of a million persons, and the man was overjoyed. Just as the man was ready to speak, Saint Peter said, "Oh, there is one thing you might like to know. Brother Noah is in the audience."

Sometimes we think we're the only ones who have ever

experienced trouble. With that view, we are prone to feel sorry for ourselves and gorge ourselves in an orgy of self-pity. Don't do it; it will lead to nothing but ruin.

The question remains: *How?* How do we handle these interruptions that life gives us?

Think About Detours as Fresh and New Opportunities.

For some of us, the detours have provided us with the most unexpected beauty of our journeys. Out of the interruptions have come new vistas and new opportunities.

On a blustery winter day in New England, Nathaniel Hawthorne was fired from his position in the customhouse of Salem. In complete discouragement, he plodded his weary way home to tell his wife the sad news of his misfortune. Her response surprised him. She told him that now he had time to write the book he always had wanted to write. This tragic detour became the opportunity of a lifetime. It was the beginning of a new career.

Many of us know the story about the people of Enterprise, Alabama. In 1910 the boll weevil came into their region from Mexico, spelling nothing but tragedy to their cotton crops. They tried and tried to find a way to overcome, but the boll weevil had the upper hand. The entire region was on the brink of economic collapse. The next year they tried a few new crops—peanuts, corn, hay, sugarcane, and sweet potatoes. To their utter amazement, they discovered that these crops would grow. In a few short years, Enterprise, Alabama, became the peanut capital of the world. Perhaps you know that these citizens built a monument with these words inscribed:

> In profound appreciation
> To the boll weevil
> And what it has done
> As the herald of prosperity

This monument was erected
By the citizens of
Coffee County
And Enterprise, Alabama

In the Bible, and in the hymn "Have Thine Own Way," we learn about the potter and the clay. Sometimes in working the clay, the potter has to stop and wait for the clay to become more pliable. This becomes a waiting time, a breathing time. John Claypool is right in saying there are some things we have to work for and some things we have to wait for. It could be that some interruptions of life are not tragedies but breathing times for us to discover new opportunities we have not had time to pursue.

Try to Learn from Detours.

Someone has suggested that the balloon is the perfect toy for children. Accidentally popping a balloon teaches them there are some things that Mommy and Daddy cannot fix. It is good to discover there are some things we cannot do. This is not negative thinking but realistically taking inventory of one's skills and abilities, which leads to learning.

Abraham Lincoln said he found success in politics by not making the same mistake twice. Henry Ford built a marvelous machine called an automobile but learned that it would move in one direction only. The next car he built had a reverse gear. He also learned that if he built a car wider than the door of the building, there was no way to get the car out without tearing down the wall. Thomas Edison said his greatest invention was the research laboratory, where he and his associates learned from their many mistakes. Babe Ruth almost became known as the strikeout king of baseball, but he learned from his hundreds of strikeouts how to hit the ball out of the park. Ed Gibson, an astronaut on the Skylab 3 mission, failed the first and fourth grades. He almost became a school dropout before he ever got started. His early difficulties became learning experiences that turned his life around. One key in handling the detours of life is to learn from our mistakes.

Trust the Lord of the Road.

Jesus knew that life would have its problems, but he warned us not to be too disturbed or concerned about the difficulties that would come: "Do not worry about your life, what you will eat, or about your body, what you will wear. . . . Consider the ravens: they neither sow nor reap, they have neither storehouse nor barn" (Luke 12:22, 24). But you cry, "The ravens sometimes fall." I know. Sometimes we also will fall. God's love for us does not protect us from life's problems. This does not mean that God has forgotten us or forsaken us. Jesus speaks of the lilies and grass of the field. Then he makes the bold declaration that if God takes care of those things, surely you will be in his love and care. God loves you. You are important to God, and you will not have to struggle alone. These are some of the most powerful words in all the Bible: "I am with you always" (Matthew 28:20).

The apostle Paul endured as many detours as anyone we have ever read about. He was stoned, beaten, shipwrecked, and imprisoned, but he still could say, "All things work together for good for those who love God" (Romans 8:28). That is difficult for us to believe when we are on the bottom side of life, but it is true. After all of Job's trouble, he declared that God had not left him.

That lesson came to one of the great composers, George Frederick Handel. In his early life he was thrown aside by the musical people of his day. That was a terrific blow. Another wave of trouble came with his father's death, which left him groping for life. He continued to write music, but no publisher was interested. He moved from Germany to England, hoping for something better, but bankruptcy ended his new dream. Having no friends or companions, he poured out his soul to God and asked for the caring that he had read about in the Bible. Many of us speak to God through words, but Handel, in that moment of absolute despondency, cried out to God through his music. It was his crying out in agony that produced the *Messiah*, which the world rejoices in today. No one can doubt that God heard his cry and gloriously responded.

Ella Wheeler Wilcox wrote those words many of us have heard or read often:

> I will not doubt, though all my ships at sea
>   Come drifting home with broken masts and sails;
>   I shall believe the Hand which never fails,
> From seeming evil worketh good to me;
>   And, though I weep because those sails are battered,
>   Still will I cry, while my best hopes lie shattered,
>   "I trust in Thee."

* * *

Detours are going to come. Interruptions will be a part of your journey. When they do come, remember these things:

- Never view a detour as the end of the road.
- Don't wallow in self-pity.
- Think about detours as fresh and new opportunities.
- Try to learn from detours.
- Trust the Lord of the road.

God has not brought you into the world for nothing. God has a dream for you. You may stumble, but God is ready to pick you up. Trust God and move on to becoming the person he wants you to be.

HOW TO ACHIEVE
GENUINE HAPPINESS

In the comic strip "Peanuts" Lucy once asked Charlie Brown if he had ever known anyone who was really happy. Snoopy suddenly appeared, interrupting her sentence. He danced across the frames of the strip with his nose high in the air and a smirk on his face, as if he owned the whole world. He gave the appearance of being deliriously happy. In the last frame of the cartoon, Lucy asked Charlie Brown if he had ever known anyone who was really happy and still was in their right mind.

Happiness is a much desired commodity. Everyone wants it—even those who seem to have all the elements of life neatly tied together.

There is a story about a young man in Paris whose life was falling apart. Something was missing. Life was not supposed to be as he was experiencing it. He went to the doctor and asked what he could do to get well. The doctor recommended he go see a man by the name of Grimaldi—the one in Paris who seemed to have everything together. Grimaldi was well known, lived in a high and mighty way, and had friends everywhere. "Go see Grimaldi," the doctor told his patient. "He will show you how to enjoy life. That will make you well." The young patient looked up at the doctor and said, "I am Grimaldi."

A questionnaire in a popular women's magazine asked one question: What will make you happy? The question was interesting because it subtly suggested that many were unhappy. Fifty-two thousand persons responded. I wonder what the response would have been if the question had been framed another way: Why are you unhappy? Can you imagine the answers?

Here are some sure-fire prescriptions for unhappiness.

1. Make little things bother you. Don't just let them, *make* them!
2. Get yourself a good worry, one about which you can do nothing but worry.
3. Be right all the time. Be the only one who is right, and be rigid about your rightness.
4. Don't trust, believe, or accept people at anything but their worst and weakest. Be suspicious of everyone.
5. Always compare yourself unfavorably to others, which guarantees instant misery.
6. Take personally, with a chip on your shoulder, everything that happens to you that you don't like.
7. Don't give yourself wholeheartedly or enthusiastically to anyone or anything.

You can perhaps add others to this list.

We know the prescriptions for unhappiness, but what are the prescriptions for happiness? Where does happiness come from? How do we find it? What must we do? Where do we begin?

We begin by acknowledging where happiness cannot be found.

Happiness Cannot Be Found in Money or Things Money Can Buy.

A newspaper offered a prize for the best definition of *money*. Out of hundreds who responded, the winner submitted the following: "Money is a universal provider of everything but happiness.'' We do not often say it aloud, but deep inside there is the feeling that money can care for all our needs. Money is important, and life could be much easier for many if there were more of it. Better housing would be a blessing for many families. A new car or boat would bring much joy to some. These things, however, are not the keys to real happiness.

Happiness Does Not Automatically Spring from Popularity or Fame.

As we watch movie stars and TV personalities emerge form their limousines into the applauding crowd, we see their smiles and somehow think they have found happiness; but applause and notoriety are not the ingredients of happiness. It is the same for many sports heroes. They are known by millions, but their fame doesn't guarantee them true happiness. They have the same problems as everyone else. Many celebrities have resorted to taking addictive drugs to cover up their misery, but the roots of unhappiness cannot be covered up.

Achievements and Accomplishments Do Not Bring Lasting Happiness.

There is much to be said for success. Finishing a project or reaching a goal is a good feeling, but this feeling does not satisfy all the emotions. Howard Hughes apparently achieved everything he ever dreamed of, but the last years of his life were spent in isolation from the world. He had many accomplishments but no genuine happiness. Jay Gould was another who achieved much but who, as he was dying, claimed to be the most miserable man on earth. Achievements and accomplishments will not solve the problem of unhappiness.

One's Surroundings Are Not the Source of Happiness.

Many people move from place to place to find happiness, but it doesn't come. They seem to think that life will be better somewhere else. Will Rogers confessed that he often grew weary of being in the same place and dreamed of greener pastures elsewhere. He said he would pick out some place that sounded good, subscribe to the local newspaper in the new town, and read that paper for a month. He then declared that he always decided not to move, because the news from the new place was no better than the news from where he was living.

Some feel their home situations hinder their happiness. They want out of their marriages. The dream for a happy home and a fulfilling relationship has been torn apart by an abusive spouse. Neglect and harassment have taken the place of care and consideration. Work schedules have left no time for together- ness. Economic pressures are more than they can bear. The children they have brought into the world may seem to interfere with their happiness. They want a change of scenery, so they scuttle everything and seek a new territory—all to no avail.

Happiness Cannot Be Found by Searching for It.

We cannot search for happiness as we search for lost car keys or a four-leaf clover. Happiness is a byproduct of a well ordered life.

A story attributed to C. L. James goes this way. A little dog was chasing its tail round and round. When a big dog asked why the little dog was acting so, the little dog replied, "I have discovered that happiness is the best thing for a dog, and that my tail is happiness. When I catch my tail, I will have happiness!"

The big dog said, "I agree that happiness is a good thing for a dog, and that happiness is in my tail. But I have found that when

I chase my tail, it escapes me. When I pay my tail no attention, it chases *me!*''

How true! Harold Kushner, author of *When All You've Ever Wanted Isn't Enough,* says that when people work on being kind, helpful, and reliable, happiness just sneaks into their lives.

If happiness does not come from money, fame, achievements, or surroundings, then where does it come from? One bumper sticker may be on target. It reads: Happiness is an inside job.

Discover the Seeds of Happiness Within You.

There is nothing external that will bring happiness. There are, of course, some surface joys—a touchdown by your favorite team, a gift from a friend, a rare find at the flea market—but these are only temporary joys. Happiness is a homegrown product. It cannot be imported from anywhere. It doesn't come from anything that happens *to* you. External circumstances are not the key ingredients. Happiness is *within* you.

Dietrich Bonhoeffer's last letter to his fiancée was written from a Nazi prison before he was hanged for his resistance to Hitler. He told her that his solitude had awakened senses in his soul that prevented him from feeling lonely or abandoned. He then asked her not to think that he was unhappy, explaining that happiness depends not on circumstances but on what is inside a person.

According to the results of the magazine questionnaire mentioned previously, 58 percent of the respondents said they suffered from depression. Forty-eight percent said they were tired. The educational and economic levels of those who answered were much above average. After an entire year of analysis, the editors discovered there was only one thing that summarized all the answers to the question, What will make you happy? It was inner peace. Happiness comes from inside.

The seeds of happiness which are within us have external expressions. To a degree greater than many want to admit, our personalities and even our faces reflect what is going on inside us. We can see love. We can see happiness. It shows in our faces.

Mark Twain said that all persons over the age of forty are responsible for how they look. This was not a negative remark; it was merely an observation that happiness shows in our faces—just as unhappiness does. How do you look? What does your face show? What story does your face tell? Someone once said that if you look like your passport picture, you probably need the trip. (If you don't have a passport, look at the picture on your driver's license!)

Happiness is outwardly expressed in many ways, but it begins within.

Germinate the Seeds of Happiness Through Purposeful Living.

Leslie Weatherhead, who preached for many years at City Temple in London, once told a story about his trip around the world on a cruise ship. One night, while he was standing on deck, he began thinking about the trip and the people on the ship. He wondered what would happen if all the passengers were told that they could enjoy all the comforts the ship had to offer but could not leave the ship, and that the crew would sink the ship when all the food and fuel were consumed. As he thought more about this, he imagined that nothing would seem different at first. Then, as the passengers began to realize their journey had no purpose—that they were sailing for no destination—they would slip over the rails, one by one, and disappear into the darkness. He concluded that life without meaning or purpose isn't worth living. Why go on living if the whole thing isn't going anywhere?

Parties and entertainment and concerts are not enough. True happiness comes through fidelity to a worthy purpose. Life demands something more than mere existence.

Living without a purpose is like playing golf without having a green or a hole. There is no fun in hitting the ball over and over and over. The fun comes in sinking the ball in the hole. There must be a purpose in hitting the ball. Likewise, there is no fun in living if there is nothing toward which you can aim. If there is no goal or purpose in your life, then you are robbed of one of life's greatest treasures.

The seeds of happiness are germinated by a life filled with purpose and direction. What is your purpose? Where are you going? Do you have a mission? Are you simply drifting about on life's ocean, or is there a port toward which you are sailing? The seeds within you are waiting for an answer.

Nurture the Seeds of Happiness by Giving Yourself to Others.

There is no happiness for those who live only for themselves. The words of scripture are well known: "It is more blessed to give than to receive" (Acts 20:35*b*). The proper translation for the biblical word *blessed* is "happy." The verse, then, might be read, "It brings more happiness to give than to receive."

How true. Human life is not intended to be consumed only in keeping the personal engine running. Real living comes when we give ourselves away. In so doing, the germinated seeds of happiness begin to grow.

Giving doesn't have to be anything extraordinary; it can be working for a worthy cause, performing a needed service, or just doing something that helps another person. True happiness comes from the knowledge that we are of some worth to the world. Someone once said that we should do something every day for others, even if it's only leaving them alone.

When the world makes its list of those who have given of themselves for others, the names of Rockefeller, Carnegie, and Vanderbilt always surface. These persons have given of themselves in remarkable ways. They have given the world hospitals, schools, social service centers, fine arts buildings, and parks. Most of us do not have the resources to do what these individuals have done, but we can be self-less givers in many other ways.

An engineer regularly does volunteer plumbing and electrical repairs for the poor. A bank president spends one night a week helping families with financial problems. A big company executive coaches a Little League baseball team. A farmer has a garden for his family and another for the community food bank. All over the country, volunteers are building homes through Habitat for Humanity. A group of elderly women sew for the Red Cross. Volunteers give hospital patients an extra touch of care. These people probably will never make the world's list of those who give of themselves, but they are finding life at its best. Giving of ourselves brings such happiness that we want to do more and more.

I once heard a story about Carey Barker, a former Washington Redskins player. One night after a game, Carey was walking in the snow to relax. He came upon a lad sitting on a curb, crying. When Carey asked the boy what was wrong, the boy told him that his dad had sent him to the store to buy a loaf of bread and he had lost the dollar his dad had given him. He was afraid to go home. Carey took the child to the store and bought the bread. As the boy started home, he said he wished Carey were his dad. Carey walked the streets that night trying to find another boy who needed a dollar and a dad.

There is no happiness for those who live for themselves. We are created for something different. The internal seeds of happiness are nourished when we give ourselves away.

Watch the Seeds of Happiness Blossom as You Build a Right Relationship to God Through Jesus Christ.

The climax to happiness is a life centered in God. Jesus said to the woman at the well: "Everyone who drinks of this water will be thirsty again, but those who drink of the water that I will give them will never be thirsty" (John 4:13, 14).

In the Bible, happiness is coming home to God, being reunited with God. For Israel it was the time of returning from exile. It was coming home to Jerusalem—to God. The Gospel of Luke tells of the happiness that came when the prodigal son returned home: "'Put a ring on his finger and sandals on his feet. And get the fatted calf and kill it, and let us eat and celebrate; for this son of mine was dead and is alive again; he was lost and is found!' And they began to celebrate" (Luke 15:22-24).

The same happiness is experienced in the parable of the lost sheep: "When he has found it, he lays it on his shoulders and rejoices. And when he comes home, he calls together his friends and neighbors, saying to them, 'Rejoice with me, for I have found my sheep that was lost.' Just so, I tell you, there will be more joy in heaven over one sinner who repents than over ninety-nine righteous persons who need no repentance" (Luke 15:5-7). The joy is the same in the parable of the lost coin. Coming to the Father is the ultimate fulfillment of life.

The apostle Paul speaks of this relationship with God as something written on his heart that nothing can take away. This is what Jesus said to his disciples as he tried to interpret his departure: "So you have pain now; but I will see you again, and your hearts will rejoice, and no one will take your joy from you" (John 16:22). Paul was a living testimony to this truth. He was shipwrecked, beaten, imprisoned, tortured, chased from one city to another, and yet he could write to the people at Philippi: "I have learned to be content with whatever I have" (Philippians 4:11). Happiness comes only when life is immersed in a right relationship with God.

Years ago the Grand Duke Alexander of Russia wrote about the conditions of his land. He questioned whether revolt could ever bring happiness to his people. He concluded that although the people's physical needs might be met, the spiritual dimension of life would be missing. Material prosperity does not bring happiness. How prophetic! Without the harmony of a relationship with God, there can be no happiness. The physical dimensions of life are not enough.

Sunshine and rain are the ingredients that produce the blossom of a flower. A right relationship with God is the ingredient that produces genuine happiness from the germinated and nurtured seed within. To God, through Jesus Christ, is the only place to go.

* * *

A man went to the doctor. The physician told him, "I'm sure I have the answer to your problem." The man answered, "I certainly hope so, doctor. I should have come to you long ago." The doctor asked, "Where did you go before?" "I went to the pharmacist," the man replied. The doctor snidely remarked, "What foolish advice did he give you?" The man said, "He told me to come see you."

Often we look for happiness in the wrong places. If you have a medical problem, see your physician. If you have a problem with your car, see a mechanic. If you have a legal problem, see your attorney. But if you want to begin a new life of happiness...

- Discover the seeds of happiness within you.
- Germinate the seeds of happiness through purposeful living.
- Nurture the seeds of happiness by giving yourself to others.
- Watch the seeds of happiness blossom as you build a right relationship with God through Jesus Christ.

In Jesus Christ you can live abundantly, and that is happiness at its best. Claim it!

V

HOW TO BE SUCCESSFUL

Success is not usually considered a Christian virtue. It is not the topic for many sermons and doesn't occupy much space in books targeted for a Christian audience. Success is most often associated with fame and fortune. Success is understood as "making it." That is not what followers of Christ talk about. Our vocabulary deals more with the merits of sacrifice and denial and surrender. But you want to be successful, and I want to be successful. Is it possible for a Christian to be a faithful disciple *and* be successful?

There was an old farmer well known for never taking a firm stand on anything. He rarely said yes or no to any concern. His reply was always, "Well, it depends on how you look at it." When talking about success, the old farmer is absolutely right. It does depend on how you look at it.

As a Christian, I wanted to understand success and how it is achieved. I began my search by visiting with several carefully selected individuals who were generally regarded as successful. My list included bankers, lawyers, corporate CEOs, city leaders, stock brokers, and a few entrepreneurs. I didn't use any forms or survey sheets but simply talked with them about the things they thought contributed to their success.

A few of them acknowledged that their families had given

them an edge by providing a good financial base for their endeavors. Some even spoke of luck—being at the right place at the right time. Still others talked about determination, commitment, dreams, vision, and focus. One confessed that the economy had turned in his favor at just the right time.

There was one visit, however, that was different. After my opening remarks, this person said, "You are visiting the wrong people. You are talking to those the community sees as successful, and they are basing their opinion on the wrong factors." He continued: "Success doesn't have anything to do with money or power or community standing. It has to do with using God-given talents toward some hope or dream that makes the world a better place. You should be talking to the school teacher who is making a difference with the children in her classroom. Why don't you interview the man down at the mission who spends his days and nights helping people out of the ditches of life? I know a widow with three children in college who works two jobs every day to keep them there. I have a man who works on the assembly line in one of our companies that has one of the best families I know. Why don't you talk to those people? They are the success stories."

In my second attempt to understand this elusive but much desired place in life, I enrolled in a management seminar on "The Secret of Success." I heard what I expected to hear, but I wanted to know more. Afterward I visited personally with the speaker, and he referred me to a company that featured Earl Nightingale on audio cassette tapes. He said this man was the "dean" of helping people find success. I found the company and listened to twenty-eight tapes that related in some way to the success subject. Finally, the moment came for which I had been waiting. I listened with excitement. I didn't want to miss a single word. Nightingale said he found the secret in an old book on his desk. What a surprise! He said the secret of success came from the Gospel of Matthew: "In

everything do to others as you would have them do to you"
(7:12a). This, he said, is the whole story of achieving success.
Forty years he searched for this answer. Amazing! Success
indeed depends on how you look at it.

My search to understand success was not a unique
adventure. This concern has been a topic of thought almost
from the beginning of time. In the book of Ecclesiastes, the
writer tells about his struggle to find success. He accumulated
great wealth; built gardens, houses, and parks; surrounded
himself with many slaves to do his bidding; gathered gold and
silver from all over the world. He even said of himself, "I
became great and surpassed all who were before me in
Jerusalem. . . . I kept my heart from no pleasure" (2:9-10).
Then he adds, "All was vanity and a chasing after wind"
(verse 11). He came to the conclusion that apart from God,
there is nothing to life.

Jesus said in unmistakable terms that life does not find
meaning in the abundance of possessions. He went on to tell a
story of a man whose land produced a huge crop. There was
such a harvest that he didn't even have room to store it. At this
point he made the decision to keep it all for himself. He would
build bigger barns and then bask in the luxury of the harvest
forever. In his mind, he had finally arrived. God didn't see it
this way and called him foolish. The rich life comes only in a
relationship to God.

Success is not something that can be possessed. It has little to
do with the points you put on the board. Success is not what one
produces or purchases but what one does to make a difference
for good. It is the fulfillment of a God-directed dream. It is
living a life of integrity. It is building a home in love. It is
building character in a child. It is operating a business with
honesty and concern for the workers. Success is fulfilling one's
potential and achieving the desire of a good heart. Success is
nothing less than faithful Christian discipleship.

The question of *how* remains. What must I do? Where do I
begin?

Accept Yourself as Someone of Worth.

When God created us, it was "very good." You are the most interesting thing God ever made. You are filled with more potential than anything God ever made. To some, you are a client, a customer, a friend, a tax payer, a student, a parent, or a child. To God, you are a magnificent example of creation at its best.

This does not mean you are a finished product. In industry, you might be described as being in the development stage. A minister once printed calling cards to read "What I am to be, I am now becoming." That is absolutely correct. We all want to be everything we are capable of becoming. You may not have reached your potential or fulfilled your possibilities, but that does not detract from your worth. Throughout your entire life, you have built-in value.

In life, we make many judgments. We make judgments about what to wear, what to eat, where to go, what careers to follow, and who to have as friends; but no judgment is as important as the one we make about ourselves. That single judgment influences everything we do by affecting our attitudes toward life. This judgment becomes the catalyst that ignites and empowers all our relationships. The relationship we have with ourselves is the most important relationship we will ever have. Dale Carnegie summed it up by saying that the best things in life come to those who appreciate themselves.

Some people have a hard time believing that success or greatness or worth can ever come to them or the people about them. That is something that happens to others in faraway places. A story is told about the Wright brothers who made the historic first flight in Kitty Hawk, North Carolina. When the word of their flight got back to their hometown of Dayton, Ohio, the editor of the newspaper reportedly refused to believe it. He said that if people were ever able to fly, it wouldn't be anyone from Dayton.

Greatness and success emerge from people who begin by

accepting themselves and their God-given abilities. You can't do everything, but Edward Everett Hale has reminded us that you can do something:

> I am only one,
> But still I am one.
> I cannot do everything,
> But still I can do something;
> And because I cannot do everything
> I will not refuse to do the something
>   That I can do.

You are someone special. Accept it. Celebrate it. This is the beginning of a successful life.

Be the Best You Can Be.

Feeling good about yourself and knowing that you are of worth unlocks the door to *being* the best you can be. For many, "doing" is the important ingredient in life, and there is no denying the importance of accomplishment. Doing connotes productivity, distance, earnings. It is a *quantity* idea. Success, however, is a *qualitative* dimension. *Being* precedes *doing*. If you measure your success only by what you produce or purchase or by what you accomplish, you are doomed to eternal dissatisfaction. There will always be someone who will outdo you. Success concerns the quality of being.

Being the *best* one can be means going all out. No one is successful who is less than he or she can be. Successful people strive for excellence in all they do. Robert Cueni in his book *The Vital Church Leader* admonishes the clergy to prepare every sermon as if it were going to be delivered on Easter morning. They should teach every class, he says, as if the apostle Paul were sitting in the back waiting to critique them. In other words, they should do everything they can do. It is no different with you. Success comes by fully using the potential God has given you. John Wooden, former coach of UCLA, said that success is the peace of mind that comes from knowing you have done your best. Nothing less will do.

The *you* is a vital part of this road to success. Some spend their entire lives wanting to be someone else. They want others' abilities or opportunities. God made you a unique individual, and you will never be the same as someone else. You were never meant to be. In *The Green Pastures,* a play by Mare Connelly, Noah says, "I ain't much, but I'ze all I got." Noah was right at one point—"I'ze all I got." But the other part was dead wrong. You are filled with a tremendous opportunity. You are someone special.

In one "Peanuts" comic strip Lucy is the psychiatrist and Charlie Brown is the patient. Lucy asks if Charlie Brown is discouraged again and if he knows what the trouble is. Before giving him time to respond, she says the trouble is that *he is Charlie Brown.* The fact that you are who you are, however, is not "trouble." The beautiful thing about you is that you *are* you. That is something to be celebrated!

Being the best you can be may involve some changes in how you prepare for your work. This is what the writer of the letter to the Hebrews had in mind when he admonished the early Christians. He spoke of those who came out to race in the stadium, surrounded by a great crowd of spectators. The writer's audience was familiar with the scene. The racers came out clothed in the lightest garments possible, because they could not run with the heavy shoes and clothes they wore every day. They put aside everything that would be a hindrance to their running. The writer envisioned heaven as the great crowd watching and then advised, "Let us also lay aside every weight and the sin that clings so closely, and let us run with perseverance the race that is set before us" (12:1).

To be your best, you may have to lay something aside. The extra weight will not be the same for everyone. Someone's downfall may be an unwillingness to forgive or some other form of sin. For another, it may be impatience or even laziness. Whatever it is that keeps you from being your best must go. This will not happen overnight, but you must dare to begin.

Being the best you can be also involves the harnessing of your mental powers—your mind. In his book *Think and Grow Rich*, Napoleon Hill says that we become what we think about. He echoes what early scholars and sages said: As you think, so shall you become. The apostle Paul put the idea in yet other words, ''Be transformed by the renewing of your minds'' (Romans 12:2). Your actions are a direct result of what is in your mind. Everything begins with a brain wave! Your life is a mirror of your thoughts. How you handle your mind is the secret to any transformation that is to take place within you.

A good attitude is essential for success. The Cox report on American business said that 94 percent of Fortune 500 executives attribute their success to attitude more than any other basic ingredient. I have never known a person to be fulfilled in life who did not have a positive attitude. Shaping attitudes begins with harnessing and handling mental powers.

God gave you the capacity to handle your thinking and control what you think about. The familiar computer phrase is appropriate, Garbage in—garbage out. If your mind is filled with impurities, then your life will ultimately reflect them. If you can determine what you think about, then it is possible to determine what you can become. You become what you think about.

Handling your mind appropriately and laying aside any hindrance will allow you to measure up to God's expectation of you. You can be all you can be.

Focus Your Life Toward Others.

Successful people are clearly focused. They know where they are going and what they are about. Many cameras have autofocus possibilities. One presses the shutter release lightly and the electronic eye moves the lens to a precise focus on the object. It is a marvelous feature. You are not so lucky—you are manually operated! Your call is to set your sights on something and let nothing deter you from it. Whatever your aim in life, singleness of purpose is essential to your success.

A well-worn story attributed to the Reverend Bob Schuller relates that he was calling on parishioners one day when he saw a great big bruising bulldog coming up the sidewalk where he was walking. All the little dogs from the yards rushed toward this old bulldog as if he were invading their territory. The old bulldog never wavered in his determined path but kept on as if nothing were happening about him. When Schuller got closer to where the old bulldog was walking, he determined that he was not going to move over for a dog. As the moment of collision drew near, it was the preacher who moved aside. The old bulldog never even paused to look him over but continued on his path as if no one were around. Later that night Schuller prayed, asking the Lord to give him whatever that bulldog had. He was asking for something that would enable him to set his mind on what he was about and never lose sight of his goal.

When writing to the church at Philippi, the apostle Paul said, "This one thing I do: [even Paul couldn't do everything] forgetting what lies behind and straining forward to what lies ahead" (3:13). There had to be a focus in his life if he were to do the one thing he wanted to do. It was the same with Jesus. He made many detours, but his course was always set toward Jerusalem.

It is no different with us. Many of us try to do too many things. Some of us are like the cowboy who jumped on his horse and rode off in all directions. Successful living comes from a life that is finely tuned and focused.

A successful life is always focused outward. It is never me-centered. This is the secret that motivational speaker Earl Nightingale discovered, who often quoted the golden rule. Success is found only in helping others. We need not concern ourselves with our own success; we need only to help others.

Jesus said that life, real life, will come only as we give ourselves away: "For those who want to save their life will lose it" (Mark 8:35). This has been a hard lesson for us to learn. Getting and keeping dominate our thoughts. Jesus' words in the Gospel of Mark tell the story: "Whoever wishes to become great among you must be your servant, and whoever wishes to be first among you must be slave of all. For the Son of Man came not to be served but to serve" (10:43-45). Woodrow Wilson said that "spiritual manhood" comes only when one realizes that it is better to serve others than to serve self. How simple! Focus your life on others, and life at its best will be yours.

Live a Committed Life.

There can be no success without commitment. Accept yourself as a person of worth, strive for being the best you can be, focus your life in the direction of others, and then give it everything you have. Commitment is more than wishing; it is more than choosing a goal. Commitment is the resolve to use your God-given potential to achieve something you feel is important.

Commitment means making hard choices. Jesus gave us a good example of this on the night he was betrayed. His prayer was the expression of a hurting soul: "My Father, if it is possible, let this cup pass from me" (Matthew 26:39*a*). There was sincerity in every word. But there was more: "Yet not what I want but what you want" (verse 39*b*).

Our choices are usually not of this magnitude, but we still have to make decisions—and some of them are not easy. The athlete has to choose the rugged exercise routine over the relaxation of the lounge chair. Another may have to choose a regulated diet instead of a lot of fatty foods. The student has to choose the hard hours of study and work over less taxing pursuits. The business person often has to choose long hours of work over the pull of the tennis court. For everyone, commitment means that difficult choices must be made.

Zig Ziglar told of a visit to the Washington Monument. As his party approached the monument, he heard the guide announcing loudly that there would be a two-hour wait for the elevator. Then the guide smiled and said there would be no wait for those willing to take the stairs. Commitment means making some hard choices.

Commitment means perseverance. When Herschel Walker was in junior high school, he was told that he was too small to play football. The coaches encouraged him to try out for track and leave football to those who were bigger. Walker did not take their advice but gave himself to an unusual regimen of exercises. He built himself into a real football hero and the winner of the Heisman trophy. When asked later about his success, he said that God had given him the ability to "stick with it" longer than anyone else. Likewise, Samuel Johnson said that perseverance, not strength, produces great works.

Years ago an energetic young employee at the Ford Motor Company sought out Henry Ford and asked how to make his life a success. Mr. Ford told him to finish whatever he started. Thomas A. Edison said the secret of his life was that he started where others left off. Perhaps none of Winston Churchill's speeches is remembered more than the one that concludes with a call to never give up.

The wide discrepancy often separating what a person started out to do and what he or she settles for can be attributed to the failure to persevere—to giving up before the required time and effort can bring the realization of earthly dreams. A person with ordinary talent and extraordinary perseverance can do almost anything. Persistent people begin their success while others end in failure.

Commitment is a life-long pursuit. I heard about a person who approached Fritz Kreisler, the world-famous violinist, and said, "I'd give my whole life to play the violin like you do."

Kreisler is said to have answered, "I have." There are no shortcuts.

Commitment is more than wishing—more than a dream or hope. Commitment is the focused determination to spend your life in the pursuit of a chosen goal. There can be no success without it.

Live in Harmony with God's Will.

There was a family with a young boy who seemed to possess unusual musical ability. At only eight years old, he was a good violinist. The family recognized his musical gifts and sought the best teacher they could find. This teacher was a retired Swiss maestro, but he accepted the task of teaching the young boy because he realized his rare ability.

For ten years the old teacher worked with the boy. The time came for his debut, and his parents booked Carnegie Hall. The hall was filled with people. From the moment he began, the young man held the crowd in the palm of his hand. They loved him. They cheered and applauded, but he ran off the stage crying. The stage manager yelled for him to get out on stage because the people were all cheering. The young man replied, "There is one who is not." The stage manager said, "All right, there is one old man who is not applauding. You can't worry about what one old man thinks when the world loves you." The violinist answered, "You don't understand. That old man is my teacher."

The world may cheer you on and applaud your every move. They may acclaim you as a success. But what about God? It is God who created you and sustained you. It is God who has a dream for you. Only by investing your life with God can you be the person God wants you to be.

In *God's Surprises,* Lance Webb tells of an event in the life of Dr. Roland Walker, a respected professor of Bible and religion. Early in his teaching, Dr. Walker grew discouraged and greatly troubled. Later he told of a night that changed his life. He couldn't sleep and got up to write this letter:

> To the Governing General of the Universe,
> Dear Sir: I hereby resign my self-appointed position as directing superintendent of my own life and of the world. I cannot level all the mountains of injustice, or fill in all the valleys of selfishness. There is too much of it in me. I hereby turn over to you for your disposition and use, my life, my money, my time and talents to be at your disposal.

Dr. Walker went to his class the next morning a new person.

The essence of success is fulfilling God's dream for your life—taking what God has given you and turning it over for God's use. Success is a byproduct of Christian discipleship. Success is not something that can be possessed—not something that can be held in your hand, or put in a bank or flaunted with a statue or marker on the city's lawn. Success is being what God wants you to be.

*   *   *

Hilda Butler Farr's "The Gift of Tomorrow" ends by reminding us that it is never too late to start:

> Tomorrow brings another chance
> For us to try once more.

God has a dream for this world, and you are a part of that dream. Like one tiny piece in a watch or an automobile, you have a part to play that is different from all others. It may be a big part or a little part, but each one is important. God gave you a life filled with possibilities. That is God's gift to you. What you do with your life is your gift to God.

- Accept yourself as someone of worth.
- Be the best you can be.
- Focus your life toward others.
- Live a committed life.
- Live in harmony with God's will.

That is success. Go for it!

VI

HOW TO DEAL WITH WORRY

Worry is one of the most critical problems facing our world today. Some have described it as the twentieth century's raging tornado. Others have likened it to the plagues of the Middle Ages. It is often called public enemy number one. It is a regular feature in most popular magazines. Worry is not a sideline issue; it is a major problem in our society, and no one is free from the ravages of its poison. It affects our total being.

Worry is a major contributor to physical illness. There are many new and marvelous breakthroughs in the medical field, but none are more important than the exploration of the relationship between our mental state and our physical well-being. Heart disease, cancer, and other physical ailments are treated by focusing on the contributing causes. Worry, anxiety, and fear are contributing factors to illnesses such as high blood pressure, stomach ulcers, headaches, thyroid disorders, and a multitude of other ailments. One physician said that 70 percent of patients could cure themselves if they could handle their fears and worries.

Worry and excessive anxiety are directly related to mental and emotional disorders. In a day when we have appliances that wash dishes and clothes, sound systems that fill the house with whatever music we desire, and conveniences of all kinds, it is strange that more than 10 percent of the beds in our health-related institutions are filled with people suffering from emotional diseases. Despondency and depression are character-istics of our time. The number of suicides is increasing every year, and no age group is left untouched.

Worry is also related to our spiritual well-being. It divides our thinking and takes us away from the central task of our living. Worry is destructive to the God-created temple, which is our body and mind. Anything that makes us less than God intended us to be is a spiritual problem.

Our world has made some remarkable advances. We have made great achievements in exploring outer space—even putting people on the moon and traveling to the far reaches of our solar system. We have created communication systems that can make an impact on our world immediately. We have become a computer-driven society with the ability to unleash information into offices and homes in a matter of seconds. We have imaging machines that can peer into the body with precision. Our accomplishments are miraculous, but we have not yet learned how to handle the basic mental power within us. Worry is still waiting to be conquered.

We must not confuse worry with concern. We should be concerned about the conditions of the world, the plight of the poor and the diseased. We should be concerned about pain in the chest or eyesight that begins to fade. Concern is a natural response when job security and family needs are at stake. It would be foolish to live without concern for what happens to us or our loved ones.

Some anxiety is natural and normal. I vividly remember the anxiety I experienced years ago at the ripe age of seventeen when I entered the Navy. I was farther from home than I had ever been. I did not know a single person there. It was more than anxiety; it was fright. A little girl getting on a bus for the first day of school has the same feeling. She is confronted with a driver who is not her father or mother, and she is riding with others she does not know. The person approaching the first day on a new job has some feeling of apprehension. A person may have anxiety over the amount of work to be done, the dinner to be prepared for guests, or the first ride to be taken on a mountain cable car. These are not worries but normal and natural anxieties.

With all that goes on about us, it's hard not to worry. We live with fear. The international scene is not stable. When one crisis is settled, another looms on the horizon. There also are problems on the domestic front. The economy goes up and down, and nothing seems constant. Jobs are scarce. People on fixed incomes have difficulty living. Broken homes and broken lives touch us all. Drugs have invaded our society with a vengeance. Alcoholism, and all the problems stemming from it, is all about us. Robberies, muggings, murders, and other abuses headline the daily news. Violence is so much a part of our day that many have barricaded themselves with bars and locks and become prisoners within their homes. These concerns cause more than anxiety. We live with fear, and fear produces worry.

With all this, Jesus says:

> I tell you, do not worry about your life, what you will eat or what you will drink, or about your body, what you will wear. Is not life more than food, and the body more than clothing? Look at the birds of the air; they neither sow nor reap nor gather into barns, and yet your heavenly Father feeds them. Are you not of more value than they? And can any of you by worrying add a single hour to your span of life? And why do you worry about clothing? Consider the lilies of the field, how they grow; they neither toil nor spin, yet I tell you, even Solomon in all his glory was not clothed like one of these. But if God so clothes the grass of the field, which is alive today and tomorrow is thrown into the oven, will he not much more clothe you. . . . Therefore do not worry." (Matthew 6:25-31)

How can we not worry? How do we deal with these gnawing fears that eat the inside of us and tear us apart?

Some do not deal with their fears at all. They wear their worries on their shoulders and won't be caught without them. They don't want to be free of worry. Their worries are the most enjoyable things they have. They relish the idea of carrying their burdens and infecting everyone they can with them.

Some try to deal with worry through excessive criticism, thinking that if they focus attention on the miserable state of others, some of their own pain will be relieved. Perhaps if they can pull others down, they will be built up. Criticizing may bring temporary relief, but negative thought compounds the existing negativism, leaving one worse than before. Excessive criticizing is a reflection of the person doing it.

Others try to handle their worry through pious self-righteousness. They convince themselves that this is the cross the Lord has put upon them, and they must bear it valiantly. Like the Pharisees, they parade this piety for all to see. It is their lot in life, and they will accept it. This piety is nothing less than blasphemy.

Alcohol and drugs become the means through which some try to escape worry. They drown themselves in addictive chemicals that wash away their thoughts and feelings. The chemicals lift them to a new high, but the high is only temporary. The effects soon wear off, and they are back where they began.

Some try to cover up their worry by adopting a rollercoaster life. They frantically fill their hours and days with activity. Like the popular batteries, they keep going and going and going. People are forever trying to cover up their worries, but this is not the answer. So how do we deal with worry?

Focus Your Life on Today.

"This is the day that the Lord has made; let us rejoice and be glad in it" (Psalm 118:24). Today is the only time you have. Whatever you are to do, whatever you are to think, whatever you are to celebrate, it will be done *today*.

When the Hebrews were wandering in the desert, people started bickering over whether they should have left Egypt with

Moses. Some wanted to return home. Food was scarce. It was under these circumstances that God taught them the secret of living for today. He provided them food daily. They could gather only what they needed for that one day and no more. They could not store any of it for tomorrow; the resources of God were available one day at a time.

Nineteenth-century writer John Ruskin had a big rock on his desk on which was carved the word *today*. It was a constant reminder that that was all he had. It was all the Hebrews had. Today is all we have.

Freedom from worry can never be accomplished if we insist on dragging the past around with us. Much of our worry is "stuff" left over from yesterday, like garbage we pull along, refusing to let go, until we can't move. Paul gave us good advice when he said, "This one thing I do: forgetting what lies behind . . . I press on" (Philippians 3:13-14). The past is past—leave it alone.

Worry cannot be solved if we insist on borrowing the anticipated problems of tomorrow. This is probably the most serious obstacle to handling worry. We insist on worrying today about what may happen in the future. Most of the things we worry about never happen. I know a woman who has worried for thirty years about having a heart attack. She said, "It runs in the family; I know I'll have one."

There is a well-worn story about a man who heard a noise in the middle of the night. He went downstairs to investigate and found a burglar emptying the silver chest. He said to the man, "Stay where you are. I want to get my wife. She has been expecting you for twenty years."

Some have dared to make a list of the things they worry about, only to discover that most of them are future events. We anticipate things that never happen. Most of the people who come to me for counseling talk about things that may be in their future. "This is the day the Lord has made." It is all we have. Focus your life on it.

Focus Your Life on the Things You Can Control.

While I was writing this chapter, the electricity suddenly went off, taking with it everything I had written on my computer screen. Since I had not finished my work, I had not made a back-up disk; everything was lost. My immediate reaction was frustration and something close to anger. I began worrying about all I had done and whether I could recapture my thoughts. Remembering that I had written about focusing on the things you can control, I could not help smiling. There was nothing I could do about this glitch in the electricity, so I had to begin again. I didn't enjoy starting over, but I had no other choice. It was something over which I had nò control.

There is much about your life you can control. You can control your schedule. (You will often declare that you can't!) You can control your work habits. You can control your personal actions and reactions. You can control your feelings toward others. There is much about your life that is in your hands—more than you think. Take charge of it, and don't fret about those things over which you have no control.

Get Control of Your Mind.

You feel and act as you think. Your mind is the center of your being. If you can control your mind, you will be turned loose to be all you can be. We've often heard that we are what we think about.

John Homer Miller once told of a woman who was unhappy with her apartment because of the noise made by the people above her. Finally she was able to get another apartment in the same building. She was so excited about finding a new place to live that her joy crowded out the old annoyances. Her mind was in her new home. When the time came to move, she decided to stay where she was. When asked about her decision, she said, "I didn't have to move into a new apartment. All I had to do was move into a new mind."

Whatever the circumstances of life, the mind can come to the rescue. Hymn writer Fanny Crosby lost her sight when only six weeks old. This could have ended her optimism for life, but her attitude took charge. When she was eight years old, she wrote:

> Oh, what a happy child I am
> Although I cannot see!
> I am resolved that in this world
> Contented I will be.
>
> How many blessings I enjoy
> That other people don't!
> So weep or sigh because I'm blind,
> I cannot, nor I won't!

Your thoughts are expressed through your actions. Take charge of your mind.

Strive for Balance in Your Life.

It is amazing to see people in foreign lands carry heavy loads upon their shoulders. My first experience of this was in Okinawa. The people would put huge loads on both ends of a pole, put the pole across their shoulders, and walk for miles. I saw the same thing in China and on a farm in Barbados. The secret, of course, is that the load is balanced. Anyone with a farming background knows the truth about balanced loads.

In the area where I live, it is not uncommon to come upon a huge truck hauling logs from the mountains. Occasionally a truck will be creeping along because the logs have shifted to one side, leaving the load unbalanced. When this happens, there is danger ahead. It is no different with your life. There is nothing more detrimental than an unbalanced life. Nerves are frayed, emotions are on edge, tempers are short, and life is chaotic.

Nature is a good example of balance. There is a season of growth and a season of rest. There is a rhythm among the atmosphere, the water, and the other elements of the environment. Likewise, a balanced life requires both activity and rest. We must sprinkle our regular routines with periods of rest and relaxation. The armed services have learned the value of R and R. There must be a time for a change of pace. When I was growing up, vacation time for workers was rare. Only the rich people took vacations. Today we know the value of these breaks. They are not just earned days off but necessary time for the body and mind to unwind and be renewed.

Vacation time, however, is just a part of the answer. There also must be day-by-day periods of rest. Many with heavy responsibilities have learned to take time daily to let their bodies and minds relax. It may be a thirty-minute snooze in the middle of the day or fifteen minutes of uninterrupted time alone. It may be a walk during the noon hour or a regular game of golf on a weekday afternoon. Occasionally Jesus grew weary and wanted to get away for rest. He knew the value of balance to a healthy life.

Variety is also a part of balance. We all have heard the saying "All work and no play makes Jack a dull boy." It is true. Life demands some activity that is different from the normal schedule. For perfect balance, there must be something on the other end of the pole. This something will be different for everyone. The letter carrier who walks a route each day may not find a long walk at night helpful. The long walk may be needed by the person sitting all day behind a desk. Not only does the paid work force need this variety; everyone needs it. The mother confined all day with small children at home needs it. Retired people need it. Variety is necessary for balance.

It is not wrong to relax, to play, or to engage in pursuits or pleasures that are not job-related. Work is noble and good, but life must have balance. Without balance, life becomes unmanageable.

Commit Yourself to Something Meaningful Outside Yourself.

There is nothing more conducive to worry than a preoccupation with yourself. For those whose entire life is centered upon themselves, there is nothing but tragedy ahead. The scripture is true: "It is more blessed to give than to receive" (Acts 20:35). Giving yourself away is not only the fulfillment of a biblical admonition, but it also is a great antidote to worry.

How you become involved with others will depend upon your circumstances—your finances, your health, and your time. There are those who find life outside themselves by financing a wing of a hospital or another institution and becoming engaged in the operation of it. Not many of us can do such things. I know of an elderly woman confined to her wheelchair who invites students from a nearby seminary to her home each week for a "family meal." This effort requires that she plan during most of the week. The meal is a marvelous contribution to the students, but it is nothing compared to what it does for her. One man cares for a rose garden at his church. Another is a volunteer at the hospital. Others serve programs of the United Way. Service in the church provides an opportunity for many. These contributions are meaningful to others, but the major benefit is to the serving individuals. Serving others gets their minds off themselves and gives them a reason for being. It puts purpose and meaning in life.

Do the Best You Can Do in Whatever You Undertake.

There is little that is more frustrating than mediocrity. No one enjoys half-done things. No good feeling comes from doing anything less than can be done. We feel a tremendous sense of accomplishment when we do the best we can do.

I do not know the worries and frustrations of much of the work force, but I do know the heartaches and anxieties of the ministry. There is a feeling of exhilaration when one enters a pulpit on Sunday morning knowing that he or she has prepared the best possible sermon. The other side of the coin is a horrible experience. To stand in the pulpit and face a congregation, many of whom come with burdens and hurts, and not be able to do the best one can do is tragic. Pastoral calls that should have been made leave one empty and troubled. Not having enough time in the day to answer the mail piled on the desk or to prepare adequately for every meeting creates an internal inferno that wrecks life.

Whether you are performing major surgery, teaching a class in history, or baking a cake for your family, do the best you can do. Half-done work is frustrating. Doing the best you can do brings joy. Remember the words of the scripture: ''I can do all things through him who strengthens me'' (Philippians 4:13).

Let God Help.

Until now, we have been considering ways each of us can do something about worry, but worry is a human weakness that cannot be conquered by human effort alone. Worry is an intrusion into God's work. We are the temples created for fulfilling God's dream on earth. We are God's children. Trying to solve our worries without God will lead only to increased worrying. God's resources are at our disposal, and God is anxious to help. "Do not worry about anything, but in everything by prayer and supplication with thanksgiving let your requests be made known to God" (Philippians 4:6). "My grace is sufficient for you" (II Corinthians 12:9). If God cares for the birds of the air and the flowers in the field, then God will surely care for us.

From my early childhood, I remember singing the words from a hymn by Charles Tindley:

> If you trust and never doubt, he will surely bring you out;
> take your burden to the Lord and leave it there.

Some plants cannot live in certain atmospheres because they will wither and die. Worry cannot live in an atmosphere saturated with a right relationship with God. It is a contradiction to have a life centered in prayer and broken apart with undue worrying. These conditions cannot exist together. Just as the eagle soaring above does not have to worry about crossing the stream below, so also the person soaring with God will be relieved of daily anxieties. Trust God to lift you out of the mire of worry into an abundant life.

In the Rocky Mountains there is a narrow, winding, and treacherous road up a mountain. There are other roads across the mountain, but many choose this narrow and rugged road because of the scenery. After choosing the road and beginning the journey, some begin to wonder if they made the right choice. The road becomes more narrow, the embankments deeper, the curves sharper—it seems impossible to continue. At just that place, there is a big sign that greets the questioning traveler. It reads: "Oh yes you can. Millions have."

*   *   *

Today many wonder if they can make it. They are not asking about a mountain road but about the fear, anxiety, frustration, and worry that inhabit their lives. It is at this point that a faithful apostle of the Lord who traveled this road before us has erected a sign. It reads:

> We know that all things work together for good for those who love God. (Romans 8:28)
> My God will fully satisfy every need of yours according to his riches in glory in Christ Jesus. (Philippians 4:19)
> Cast all your anxiety on him, because he cares for you. (1 Peter 5:7)
> Do not worry about anything, but in everything by prayer and supplication with thanksgiving let your requests be made known to God. (Philippians 4:6)
> I will never leave you or forsake you. (Hebrews 13:5)
> The Lord is my helper; I will not be afraid. (Hebrews 13:6)

Keep these words in your mind and heart, and remember that you can free yourself from worry if you will . . .

- Focus your life on today.
- Focus your life on the things you can control.
- Get control of your mind.
- Strive for balance in your life.
- Commit yourself to something meaningful outside yourself.
- Do the best you can do in whatever you undertake.
- Let God help.

When you and God are working together, you can live without worry!

VII

HOW TO COPE WITH GRIEF

In a "Peanuts" cartoon Charlie Brown is walking away from the baseball game with his head down, feeling totally dejected. When he comments to Lucy that he is tired of losing, she reminds him that we learn more from losing than from winning. That doesn't help Charlie Brown at all. His response is that he must be the smartest person in the world.

My interest is not in arguing the merits of winning or losing but in affirming that losing is routine. It is estimated that 10 percent of the population is constantly involved in some kind of major crisis. If you are not a part of this 10 percent, hold on—your time will come. There is no immunity from grief; grief is no respecter of persons. Some things in life can be avoided through education, wealth, or position, but not grief. Someday, in some way, your life will be interrupted with a blast. For most of us, grief already has made regular visits into our life.

Someone has said that grief is the agony of an instant and the indulgence of grief is the blunder of a lifetime. There is no doubting that grief is a sudden agony. If the handling of grief can become one of life's blunders, how should we deal with it?

Recognize That There Are Many Sources of Grief.

We must first recognize that grief springs from many different types of soil. Most of us think of grief as the agony caused by the death of a loved one, but death is not the only source of grief. Grief is triggered by a variety of events, and grieving is a part of every one of them.

Grief comes from separation and divorce. A woman said while shedding tears of grief, "I have invested twenty-eight years of my life in my marriage. Now it's gone—along with the best years of my life." Whatever the condition, separation from those with whom we have spent a portion of our lives is painful. Separation and divorce often distance us from those we have accepted into our families—the in-laws and friends made through the marriage. When couples separate or divorce, one parent usually takes the children, allowing the other parent visiting privileges only. Spouses often experience a loss of personal identity and position in the community. Unlike death, however, separation and divorce do not bring finality to relationships. The once-partners may see each other on the street or in church. Face-to-face encounters occur when visitation rights are exercised.

Grief caused by separation and divorce is increased by anxiety about the future. Couples are plagued by questions such as "Now what?" "How am I to live?" "Where will I find work?" "How can we adequately support the children?" and "What about our mutual friendships?" They may feel angry, lonely, and abandoned. Some declare this is grief at its worse.

For some, retirement is a time of grief. Their identity has been their work, and suddenly it's gone. Their friends are at the plant or in the office. Their lives are centered in the classroom with the children where they have spent years teaching. They have gone to work every morning for thirty or more years, and,

73

suddenly, there is no place to go. Retirement leaves them adrift without direction or meaning. They have no one to affirm them as persons, as they once had. Retirement for some is a glorious experience, but not for everyone.

The abrupt termination from a job is often a grief experience. A friend came by my house one afternoon with a heart as heavy as anyone I have ever seen. He had given his life to a company where he was a manager. The company merged into another company, and the new people determined they did not need him. He was in his middle years and had expected that position to be his life's work. He was set adrift. Where was he to go? What was he to do? How would he face tomorrow? This is grief.

For a few, aging brings grief. Some people can't accept themselves because they are not as they once were. They can't do the things they once could do. An elderly friend of mine plays golf frequently. That may seem to be good, but, for him, it is tragic. I don't know why he continues to play. He plays a good game—far better than I have ever played; but, because he can't score as he once did, he becomes frustrated and irritable every time he plays. He can't accept the fact that he is not what he used to be. Age brings physical and mental changes, and some can't handle the changes.

Grief comes from our mobile society—from the uprooting of family. Grief comes when one loses a house to wind or fire, or when one has to move because of a loss of eyesight or hearing. Financial reversals bring grief. Older people face grief when they have to part with their lifetime possessions and move into a retirement center or nursing home. There is a tinge of grief when one's homeplace is gone. Mother and Father have died, and the home where all one's younger years were spent is sold. In these and many other ways, we experience the grief of change.

Grief comes into our lives in a multitude of ways. Although the effects of grief are different in each case, an understanding of what is happening helps us to deal with the grief.

Understand the Stages of Grief.

Granger Westberg, in his book *Good Grief*, says there are ten possible stages or levels through which one normally passes when dealing with grief. Robert Dodd, in *Out of the Depths,* deals with grief in another way but also insists that grief is not a one-emotion experience. Although we do not experience grief in the same way or pass through the same stages of grief, we can identify several major stages of grief.

Grief usually begins with a feeling of shock or disbelief. We go through a period of denial. ''This can't be happening to me,'' we say. For the moment, we are anesthetized. It is a human escape mechanism. Usually denial is a temporary feeling, but it may last for days or weeks.

Sometimes grief turns into a quest for revenge. We want to strike out at someone or something. It may be the surgeon who didn't save our loved one or the ambulance driver who didn't arrive soon enough. We may harbor ill feelings toward the nurse who was out of the room when our loved one died. We hurt, and our grief leads us to believe that someone is to blame.

Loneliness is often a part of the grief experience. Like Ezekiel, we have the feeling that no one has ever experienced anything like what is happening to us. During these times we don't even feel God is near. The psalmist felt this often: ''How long, O Lord? Will you forget me forever? How long will you hide your face from me? How long must I bear pain in my soul, and have sorrow in my heart all day long?'' (Psalm 13:1-2).

Guilt is often experienced during grief. A mother lashes out, ''If only I had not left her bedside!'' A daughter regrets permitting her mother to drive when she knew better than to let her do it. ''I should have stopped him from climbing up on the house!'' someone cries. The grieving person often assumes responsibility for what has happened.

At times, grief may bring physical or emotional illness. Breathing becomes difficult. We feel dizzy or faint. Our throat begins to close. We have tightness in our chest. Our stomach begins to cramp. Sleep is impossible. These symptoms are not simply something happening in our minds; they are real.

Occasionally, grief will lead to a state of panic. Life is not as it once was. Decisions are difficult, the pieces do not fit, and the mind is not clear. It is hard to concentrate. Panic takes over. We think we are losing our minds.

The stages of grief vary with the source of the grief, our own maturity, and our faith. Some may first experience panic or physical discomfort. Others may feel a sense of guilt from the past. Sometimes loneliness or depression is the first sign of grief. It is important to know that these stages are a part of grief; they are normal reactions. We may stay in one stage longer than another, or we may pass through several stages without any problem; but we all deal with grief as a process.

Because hurt and loss are multifaceted experiences, it helps to understand what is happening when grief comes upon us. Now, what are we to *do* when grief comes upon us? How are we to cope with grief?

Acknowledge and Accept the Situation.

Freud and other psychiatrists have referred to grief as work. It's tough. The beginning is acceptance; and until this happens, no healing can take place. Loss and hurt, coming from whatever source, must never be "covered up." A prescribed medication of some kind may help one initially to cope with a traumatic experience, but medication does not lead one to acceptance.

I often have been present when death occurs. One night I stood with a wife, holding onto her hand and the hand of her husband as he breathed his last. I knew he was gone, and she knew it too. We didn't have to wait for the attending physician, yet she cried, "No, no . . . it can't be! I don't believe it!"

This refusal to accept loss usually is an immediate reaction but often is seen long after a death or separation has occurred. Denial may be expressed by refusing to move or get rid of anything in the house that belonged to the loved one. The office is closed, and nothing is to be moved. The desk is left exactly as it was, and no drawer is to be opened. The closet is never touched. The piano is closed, never to be played again. These are expressions of a lack of acceptance. The separation or death already has happened, but not for the one remaining. Lack of acceptance is more common when the loss comes through accident or tragedy, because there has been no anticipation of death.

One day Linus and Charlie Brown were chatting. Linus said that avoiding problems is the best way to solve them. He shared his philosophy with Charlie Brown: Any problem, regardless of size or complexity, can be run away from. This is not true for grief. You can't run away from it. Grief must be accepted.

Myra Welch's poem "The Touch of the Master's Hand" is a beautiful poem about what God can do with a life. It was only after a severe loss that confined her to a wheelchair that Myra Welch found a new life. She didn't give up. The acceptance of her loss started the process of a new life. Helen Keller thanked God for her handicaps, because through them she found herself, her work, and her God. The first step in dealing with grief is to accept the loss bringing the hurt.

Let It Out.

Grief must be expressed in some way. Without release, grief often results in emotional or physical problems. It is estimated that one out of every ten persons in mental institutions today is there because of repressed grief. The expression of grief will vary from person to person according to the problem. Your expression of grief will be determined by who you are and the way you naturally release your emotions. Some will cry—that's all right. Others do not cry easily; their emotions have other outlets. Nevertheless, in some way, the hurting must be expressed.

In biblical days, there were prescribed ways for grief to be expressed. For three days there was to be weeping and wailing. For a week, the deceased were eulogized by members of the community. Those in grief stayed in their homes. They wore dark clothes, without jewelry or ornamentation, for a month. If the deceased was a parent, there would be no expression of joy for a year.

Our culture does not expect such rigorous expressions, but some of us remember when those who were grieving wore dark clothes during a period of mourning. Many women in mourning also wore veils. I am not suggesting we return to the practices of earlier years, but I am suggesting we find our own ways to express grief. Without some release, grief will settle inside, bringing havoc into our lives.

Emotional release usually is harder for men than for women. Men are programmed from early childhood not to cry. Little boys are told they shouldn't cry; crying is bad. But crying has nothing to do with gender; it is a built-in emotional release.

Of course, crying is not the only emotional release. Some find release through spiritual reflections. Others find help by talking with friends or family. Still others draw strength from being alone and pondering the blessings of the past. The Scriptures and hymns of the faith provide solace to some. I know a woman who found release by taking up the work of the person for whom she was grieving. Whatever is helpful to you, do it. *Let it out*.

A word of caution: Be honest when expressing your emotions. Expressing a facade of grief will only result in guilt. Putting on a "brave face" will only hide your grief and delay the process. Stoicism may seem admirable, but it is merely a coverup. Hurt and loss must be expressed in some way, and that expression should be genuine.

Let Others Help.

Others cannot solve your problem for you. They cannot take away the loss or hurt, but they can support you in your time of grieving. Often hurting people bottle their feelings inside themselves; and, like a cyst, the infection gets bigger and bigger. Don't be afraid to let others touch your life.

Let the church community help you. Many times I have seen healing come to those who gathered with others during times of worship and Bible study. These people are your friends. They are the people with whom you have committed a life of service to the Lord. Drink from this well. Jesus said that those who would drink the water that he would give would thirst no more. Believe it. One woman said the first ray of hope for her came when she held the Communion glass in her hand and realized that God was present and her friends were around her.

Sometimes it helps to share your feelings with a true friend who will listen and talk. Often it is enough just to be with someone. There is a story of a little girl who had suffered the loss of a girl friend. Upon arriving home, the little girl's mother asked where she had been. She said she had been at the home of her friend's mother, comforting her. Her mother asked, "How could you comfort her? What did you say?" The child replied, "I didn't say anything. I just sat in her lap and cried with her." Is there anyone who would not believe that comfort was given and received?

Today there are support groups of all kinds in most communities. Alcoholics Anonymous groups led the way in offering support to those who were hurting from the problem of alcoholism. Persons active in Alcoholics Anonymous can relate to one another because they understand what is happening to one another. The same phenomenon occurs in support groups for those who are grieving—such as groups for those who are divorced, who are in the midst of career changes, or who are retired. These groups do not focus on lectures but provide encouragement and support.

It may be that you require the help of a professional counselor—a pastor, a psychologist, or a psychiatrist. Grieving is not as simple as some think. Grief results from a major interruption of life and may require serious treatment. Seeking the help of a professional is not a bad reflection on you but a statement about your good judgment.

Draw upon the Resources of God.

Like nature, life has its seasons. "For everyone there is a season, and a time for every matter under heaven: a time to be born, and a time to die; . . . a time to weep, and a time to laugh; a time to mourn, and a time to dance; . . . a time to seek, and a time to lose" (Ecclesiastes 3:1-6). Knowing the seasons, Jesus said, "Blessed are those who mourn, for they will be comforted" (Matthew 5:4). Jesus, who is fully aware of our situations, bursts forth with the bold declaration that grief doesn't have to be handled alone. The resources of God are adequate for every need.

Regrettably, God and Christianity are probably maligned more during a struggle with grief than at any other time. Our faith is essential in dealing with grief, but it must not be misinterpreted or misused. Occasionally this misuse is self-inflicted, but, most often, it comes from well-meaning friends seeking to bring comfort. There are at least three distinct falsehoods that can prevent us from drawing upon the resources of God.

1. *If you have faith, you will not grieve.* I have heard people seeking to bring comfort to a friend say, "You must not grieve. You are a person of faith." Jesus had faith such as the world had never seen, but he grieved over the death of Lazarus. Though he had the power to change life for those who hurt, he hurt *with*

them. He even hurt for those who were putting him to death. Grieving is not contrary to faith.

2. *Suffering is a consequence of wrong.* In the Old Testament there is much that relates loss and suffering to sin. The argument of Job's friends was that his misfortune could not be happening if there were not sin in his life. They said, "If you will seek God and make supplication to the Almighty, if you are pure and upright, surely then he will rouse himself for you and restore to you your rightful place" (Job 8:5-6). Job's friends were saying that a right relationship with God brings protection from such evil. Good people do not suffer.

In Jesus Christ, God's heart was perfectly revealed. From him we know that suffering, hurt, and loss are not always the result of personal sin. Jesus suffered as no one has ever suffered, and there was no sin in his life. The apostle Paul lived with suffering. The early church was born of suffering, pain, and death. The early Christians were not spared. The Christian religion never has been granted immunity from hurt and loss. Jesus asked those who requested a special place in his kingdom if they could suffer enough for such a place: "Are you able to drink the cup that I am about to drink?" (Matthew 20:22). The idea that suffering is a result of sin persists, but suffering is not the direct consequence of sin.

3. *Suffering and loss are God's will.* When we ascribe suffering and mourning to God's will, we are holding God responsible. We are saying that it's God fault. We don't say it in those words, but that is what we mean.

I have heard friends seeking to console a grieving person say, "God wanted your mother, or he would not have taken her." Following a tragic accident, I overheard these words, "If this had not been God's will, it would not have happened." Sometimes the consoling words are more general: "This is God's will, and you must accept it." Parents are sometimes told, "God wanted more little angels in heaven, and he chose your baby to be at his side." Occasionally one will hear, "God didn't want your little boy to have to endure all the sufferings that come with later life." I have even heard, "God has brought this to you so that you will grow a stronger Christian character."

What does all this say about God? Apparently there is comfort in believing that grief is the result of divine providence. A wise person once said, "I will protect myself from my enemies, if the Lord will protect me from my friends."

I have probably given more than a hundred copies of Leslie Weatherhead's *The Will of God* to grieving and hurting families. In this book Weatherhead describes God's intentional will, circumstantial will, and ultimate will. God allows things he does not cause. It is not God's will that we should suffer and hurt and grieve, but he permits our suffering. God created us for freedom, and the exercise of this freedom brings consequences that we must bear. God can step into the world and alter circumstances any time he chooses—and he does—but usually we live with the freedom he has given.

Christianity is not a fetish that protects us from the ills and disasters of the world; to be such would be a contradiction of the freedom God has given us. Christians fall and stumble just as everyone else does. Our religion is not a protective shield; it is a source of strength that sustains us through times of trial. However we seek to handle our grief, nothing compares to the strength we draw from God. We find healing in God.

God's love is sure. We sometimes may doubt the love of others, but there can be no doubting God's love. God's love is for everyone—the good and the bad alike. There is nothing that will change God's love for us.

A New England farmer put a weather vane on top of his barn that bore the inscription "God is Love." A neighbor asked him, "What do you mean, putting such words on a weather vane? Do you mean that God's love is as unpredictable as the wind?" "Oh no," replied the farmer, "I mean that God's love is sure, whichever way the wind is blowing."

The psalmist knew this love of God: "Where can I go from your spirit? Or where can I flee from your presence? If I ascend to heaven, you are there; if I make my bed in Sheol, you are there. If I take the wings of the morning and settle at the farthest limits of the sea, even there your hand shall lead me, and your right hand shall hold me fast'' (Psalm 139:7-10). There is no way we can be outside or beyond the presence and love of God.

The apostle Paul was writing to the church at Rome. Christians there were experiencing great trouble. He wrote:

> What then are we to say about these things? If God is for us, who is against us? . . . Who will separate us from the love of Christ? Will hardship, or distress, or persecution, or famine, or nakedness, or peril, or sword? . . . No, in all these things we are more than conquerors through him who loved us. For I am convinced that neither death, nor life, nor angels, nor rulers, nor things present, nor things to come, nor powers, nor height, nor depth, nor anything else in all creation, will be able to separate us from the love of God in Christ Jesus our Lord. (Romans 8:31-39)

God's help is assured. When Shadrach, Meshach, and Abednego were confronted with the fiery furnace, they declared to the king, "If our God whom we serve is able to deliver us from the burning fire and out of your hand, O king, let him deliver us. But if not, be it known unto you, O king, that we will not serve your gods" (Daniel 3:17-18).

What assurance the psalmist gives us: "I lift up my eyes to the hills—from where will my help come? My help comes from the LORD, who made heaven and earth" (121:1-2).

Jesus said, "Come to me, all you that are weary and are carrying heavy burdens, and I will give you rest. Take my yoke upon you, and learn from me; for I am gentle and humble in heart, and you will find rest for your souls" (Matthew 11:28-29).

Clearly Jesus wants us to come to him for help. God has always been available to help in time of trouble. It was never God's intention that we should face the trials of life alone.

God's healing power can be trusted. We live with trust in other arenas of life. We trust the pilot who flies the plane, the driver at the wheel of the automobile, and the one holding the rope while mountain climbing. Surely we can trust the God who created and sustains the world. The words of Charles Wesley's hymn "Jesus, Lover of My Soul" are the expression of a heart that trusted the power of God to heal.

> Other refuge have I none,
> hangs my helpless soul on thee;
> leave, ah! leave me not alone,
> still support and comfort me.
> All my trust on thee is stayed,
> all my help from thee I bring;
> cover my defenseless head
> with the shadow of thy wing.

Perhaps the most important time to remember that God has the power to heal any hurt is upon the loss of a loved one. Those who are grieving or will grieve over the loss of a loved one must remember that *death does not mark the end of life*. One of my seminary professors used to say that death is the comma in the sentence; it is not the period marking the end. The comma indicates that something more is ahead. Christ has abolished death, and the glory of eternal life with God awaits those who have claimed life in him. "Death has been swallowed up in victory" (1 Corinthians 15:54).

George Matheson's hymn speaks of death as giving back to God what was already his. God does not take life away; rather, we relinquish our hold on life and offer it to God so that eternity may be more complete.

> O Love that wilt not let me go,
> I rest my weary soul in thee;
> I give thee back the life I owe,
> that in thine ocean depths its flow
> may richer, fuller be.

Jesus' words from the Gospel of John assure us of this victory: "Do not let your hearts be troubled. Believe in God, believe also in me. In my Father's house there are many dwelling places. If it were not so, would I have told you that I go to prepare a place for you? And if I go and prepare a place for you, I will come again and will take you to myself, so that where I am, there you may be also'' (14:1-3).

There is no help for the grieving person as the help that comes from the Lord. God's love for us is sure. Because God is fully able to help, we should trust him.

In his book *The Christian and His Sorrows*, Dr. W. A. Smart related a story from a surgeon. A father brought into the surgeon's office a little girl with a cut near her eye. It was not serious, but the location of the injury made it important that it be fixed properly.

The doctor decided a couple of stitches were needed, but he didn't want to give the child an anesthetic. He explained what he wanted to do and asked the child if she could stand it. She said she could, if her father would hold her hand. The father then took her in his lap, slipped his arm around her, and held her tight. The doctor did his work, and the little girl never flinched.

The father could not possibly have erased the pain from the sutures; but if the father had not been there, the girl's reaction probably would have been much different. Dr. Smart concluded by saying that this simple illustration suggests the experiences of thousands of God's children. Like little children, we can slip our hands into God's hand and find peace and strength—regardless of how dark or painful the way may be.

* * *

When grief disrupts your life and your world . . .

- Acknowledge and accept the situation.
- Let it out.
- Let others help.
- Draw upon the resources of God.

Jesus said he would be with us, and that is enough!

VIII

HOW TO MANAGE LONELINESS

Loneliness is no respecter of age or status; very few escape it. Loneliness is one of the plagues of life. More than 75 percent of people are affected by this malady sometime during their lives. Contrary to the generally held view that loneliness is experienced only by the elderly, loneliness is a reality for more of us than want to believe it. If left unattended, loneliness can lead to physical, mental, and spiritual trauma.

Whatever the cause, the feeling of being alone is a frightening experience. After Elijah had overcome the priests of Baal on Mount Carmel, Jezebel threatened to take his life within the next few hours. He fled the country, went a day's journey into the wilderness, and cried out in desperation, "O God, take my life. . . . I alone am left" (1 Kings 19:4, 10). In *The Rime of the Ancient Mariner,* the cry sounded for all: "Alone, alone, all, all alone." The news media covered the story of three persons lost at sea with little water and practically no food. When asked about their ten-day ordeal, they reported that the most devastating part of their experience was being all alone in an ocean that seemed as big as the world.

Loneliness is more than mere isolation. We can experience loneliness in crowds as well as in the wilderness or on the ocean. City life has been described as a million people being lonesome together. One of my most memorable lonesome moments came the first night away from home in a Navy boot camp barrack filled with other sailors.

We also experience loneliness when we suffer the loss of a companion. Some of us have not yet had this experience and thus cannot fully feel the grief and pain of separation. Nursing homes are filled with many who are lonely because they are separated from familiar surroundings. When our lives are drastically interrupted by circumstances, we experience loneliness.

This emotional infection also attacks those whose shoulders bear heavy responsibilities. Many people in government and business carry tremendous burdens. They may have financial resources and be surrounded by people, but the weight of their work is heavy. Their employees and the shareholders of the company depend on them. Some government leaders have to make decisions that influence the entire world. The well-known words haunt them: The buck stops here.

Life is also heavy for those who are not leaders. A cartoon showed a huge desk with an executive sitting behind it. Undoubtedly this man was the manager or owner of the company. A laborer, standing on the other side of the desk, said to his boss, "If it's any comfort, it's lonely at the bottom too!"

The single parent with children has responsibility for the early-morning day-care delivery, the school car pool, the stressful job, the family meals, and the housework. The next day it starts all over again. It never stops, and the light at the end of the tunnel seems to have disappeared.

Loneliness is experienced by those who feel compelled to take stands contrary to those taken by their friends, whether in the political arena or religious life. It's not easy to buck the tide of popularity. Being "different" is particularly tough for young people, because acceptance by peers is important to them. To stand alone when the crowd goes in another direction is a bewildering experience. Making decisions that are unpopular brings a feeling some of us would just as soon miss.

Many people feel isolated when life doesn't shape up according to their dreams. Alcohol and drugs have turned some lives inside out when things have not turned out as expected. Many disappointments can produce a terrible sense of being alone—not making the cheerleading team, missing the cutoff for the football team, failing the entrance exam for long-awaited law school.

Fear breeds loneliness. A young girl suffers abuse from her father. She grows up with a fear of men and finds relationships with males difficult to manage. She can't shake the experiences of the early years. A business executive is betrayed by some of his managers. From this experience he develops a fear of trusting anyone. He builds a wall around himself and will not let others into his life or business.

Loneliness is no respecter of persons. It afflicts children, youth, adults in the prime of life, and the aging. There are very few who will be untouched by loneliness in their life. Is there a prescription that can bring a cure? Is there a way to overcome loneliness? Because we are susceptible to loneliness, how do we manage it?

Diagnose the Cause.

The first step in overcoming an illness is to diagnose it. It is difficult to treat something if we are uncertain of it. What are the causes of loneliness? Where did loneliness come from, and what has been its effect?

A woman in her middle years was having trouble loving her husband in the way she felt she should. She could not trust him or give herself to him. It was affecting their marriage, and she knew it was her fault. Through the help of a counselor, she discovered the problem. She had grown up adoring her father, but one day he mysteriously abandoned his family. Unconsciously she had carried the fear that if she ever loved another man, he would leave her. Understanding the problem made her life different.

A young boy grew up in a home where his father's business required the family to move almost every year. Again and again the lad would make friends, only to leave them. Losing the friendships he had developed became increasingly painful, and he began withdrawing from people. He would not allow himself to be close to anyone. This loneliness continued in his adult life, costing him job after job. A diagnosis turned his life around. He discovered the cause of his problem.

Often the cause of one's loneliness is known immediately. A single mother with small children to care for feels trapped. She is so busy with all her responsibilities that her need for companionship cannot be met. Another person's life is drastically changed by the isolation of divorce or illness. In such instances, the problem is apparent.

Loneliness can be handled if one knows the cause, but sometimes the cause is not apparent. Asking questions may help to determine the cause. Is there a communication problem? Are there feelings of inadequacy? Is there hostility? Is there fear? Has there been a lingering time of grief? Have the circumstances of life been overpowering? Understanding the cause is the beginning of an answer.

Cultivate the Friend Inside You.

A wise man once said that if he lost every friend on earth, he still would have the friend inside him. The flame of life never goes out where there is love, and love begins with respect and appreciation for oneself. There is, of course, a love for self that is ugly and sinful, but a healthy regard for oneself is a highly desirable quality.

Some people do not like themselves. They yearn to be tall but are short. They want to be thin but are fat. They want to sing like another but can't carry a tune. They want to dance like others but have no rhythm. They dream of being athletic but lack coordination. They spend their lives wanting to be something different, and this leads to personal frustration and hostility toward themselves.

Bill Luffburrow told a story about two elderly sisters who bought a house beside a road and put up a sign that read "Antiques." People would stop, and the sisters would serve tea and cookies mixed with much enjoyable conversation. Later the visitors would ask to see the antiques. The sisters would eagerly answer, "You're looking at them." They didn't bemoan their age. They accepted it and, apparently, had a good time with it!

God has given you a mind and a body loaded with ability. You may not be like others. Indeed, you *are* not. You are a unique individual. Remember, though, that God did not create you as a finished product. He gave you seeds to be planted and nurtured, and opportunities to challenge your best. You are someone. Celebrate it!

You can have a good friend inside you. You can be by yourself and not be lonely. Accept yourself and love yourself. You will find yourself good company throughout your life.

Find Support Through Others.

Though we have a friend inside us, we are created for additional companionship. Buried deep inside us is a longing for contact with others, for belonging somewhere—being accepted, loved, and wanted. Mother Teresa said that the most widespread disease today is the feeling of being unwanted.

When Speaker of the House Sam Rayburn discovered his serious illness, he surprised his colleagues by announcing he was going back to his home in Bonham, Texas. Why would he do that? they asked. Why go to such a place for medical treatment when the best medical facilities in the world are available in Washington, D.C.? Mr. Rayburn told them he was going home because the people of Bonham, Texas, know when you are sick and care when you die.

The Alcoholics Anonymous program was founded by a recovering alcoholic who asked some of his alcoholic friends to visit with him when he was tempted to resume his drinking. Because of his problem, he felt isolated from society, and he needed friends who would accept him and not be judgmental. From that casual, unplanned meeting, a great support movement was begun.

All of us need such a group. Groups for divorced people are providing a fellowship that understands and accepts those who are recently divorced. Singles groups are springing up everywhere. Cancer support groups, heart transplant groups, and other health-related groups are meeting a great need. The Boy Scouts and Girl Scouts serve the same purpose. Church fellowship groups are answering the needs of people. Civic organizations also provide help. Belonging is a part of our basic nature. Everyone needs to be known and cared about.

In his autobiography, Robert Brooke told of a trip he made from England to America aboard the ship *C. C. Cedric*. When he arrived at the dock, he noticed that all the people seemed to have someone there to see them off except him. In the midst of the hugging and kissing and saying goodbye, Brooke said he felt very much alone and out of place. He saw a young boy nearby, called him over, and asked if he would like to earn a few shillings. The boy said he would and asked what he needed to do. Brooke told him to wave to him as he left. As the ship pulled away, there stood the little boy, waving with all his might, and Brooke waving back. Everyone needs somebody.

Many incarcerated persons experience the need for recognition and caring. One young man having difficulty with prison life asked to see a minister. The clergyman arrived and asked what he could do for him. He said, "Talk to me. Talk to me like

I'm somebody. Say my name, please say my name. I'm somebody too.''

Belonging, being accepted, being known—these are as important for life as food and drink. We are living in a day of fantastic systems of communication, but there is no TV show, radio program, book, or anything else that can replace human relationships. We are made for relationship with others, and life cannot be meaningful without it.

Do Something for Others.

It is a joy to receive, but the Scripture is correct: The greatest happiness comes from giving. Albert Schweitzer, the great missionary physician to Africa, advised us to do something "free of charge" for someone every day. There is nothing that nourishes and enriches life as much as the sharing of ourselves with others—especially when it is freely given.

Service for others can take many forms. I know an elderly artist who teaches painting at her church to those who would like to see what they can do with the brushes and colors and canvas. Her life, and theirs, is enriched by her sharing. Another person delivers meals-on-wheels. He doesn't have to do it; he has plenty of other things to do. But in feeding others, he is feeding himself. Making the rounds of his "clients" is one of his happiest times. Every church has visits to be made, or a phone to be answered, or a library to be kept, or flowers to be arranged. Some people visit nursing homes. Others volunteer at the hospital. Some coach ball teams or serve on the volunteer fire department.

Some will quickly disqualify themselves from this kind of activity by making excuses. They can't deliver meals because they do not have transportation. They can't coach the ball team or teach art because they lack the necessary skills.

A young man hitched a mule and a horse to a wagon. A friend

said to him, "My father said never to hitch a mule and a horse together." The other boy said, "My father said to do the best you can with what you have."

No one can do everything, but each of us can do something. Making a difference in the lives of others will make a difference in you. It is a potent medicine for a hurting and lonely soul.

View Life Through a Wide-angle Lens.

Your lifetime and mine are not the whole of human existence. We are a part of a continuing history. Ralph Waldo Emerson reminded us, "Every man is an omnibus on which all of his ancestors are seated." How, then, can we ever be lonely when we have such an invisible company always around us? Our ancestors are in us—they are a part of our lives.

I was privileged on two occasions to be the week-long speaker at a family reunion. Most family gatherings last an afternoon or a day, but this one is always for a full week. The family has been assembling at the same place for more than a hundred years. They come from all over the world, bringing together three or four hundred people. A part of the annual ritual is to teach the children about the family. The family tree now has many branches, but everyone knows where he or she belongs on it. Family members tour the cemetery to remember those who have gone before. They visit the ancestral homes to see the places where early family members lived and worked. They gather each night in the family-branch groups to relate the well-worn family stories. This family has a sense of belonging to something bigger than just today. They are a part of a larger family, surrounded by generations of people who are a part of their lives.

Our lives are not lived in isolation. We are a part of a continuing history. Today is connected to the past, and that past is part of us.

Remember You Are Never Alone.

Life is often accompanied by a dreadful feeling of isolation and loneliness. A young boy feels it when he is rejected by his parents. A wife feels it when she realizes she must face life without her husband. The elderly feel it when they are uprooted from their home to enter a nursing facility. The business woman feels it when the company collapses and she is without resources. These situations bring a fear that is almost unbearable.

This is the feeling that Jesus experienced when he was with the disciples in the Upper Room. He was thinking of the future and how he would face it. His words reflect his thoughts: "The hour is coming, indeed it has come, when you will be scattered, each one to his home, and you will leave me alone" (John 16:32*a*). It is a strange and frightening experience to discover you are all alone.

If that were the end of the story, we would be filled with dejection and loneliness, but there was more. Immediately after Jesus fell into that dreadful thought of the disciples leaving and his being all alone, there came a triumphant note: "Yet I am not alone because the Father is with me" (John 16:32*b*).

God being with us is the greatest news ever given. It brings the possibility of a new life. It puts meaning into all we do and reorients our life. We sense a newfound joy. This was the experience of the shepherds in the field on that memorable night of Christ's birth: "Emmanuel!" God is with us. On the Emmaus road, after the crucifixion, everything was lost for Cleopas and his companion. There was no hope. They were all alone—until that moment when they heard the words, "He's alive! He's alive."

All of us have heard the sounding of "Taps." Some of us remember the feeling of hearing it at Army camp or aboard a ship at sea. Others remember it from a cemetery as a body was lowered into a grave. The notes call us to a moment of serious contemplation, but it is a triumphant sound—we are not alone.

Day is done, gone the sun,
From the lake, from the hills, from the sky,
All is well, safely rest,
God is nigh.

When the color fades from the sky of life and darkness is all about us, what an assurance to hear, "God is nigh." Jesus said, "Peace I leave with you; my peace I give to you. . . . Do not let your hearts be troubled, and do not let them be afraid" (John 14:27). He also said, "I am with you always, to the end of the age" (Matthew 28:20).

With this assurance you can declare with the psalmist:

Where can I go from your spirit?
    Or where can I flee from your presence?
If I ascend to heaven, you are there;
    if I make my bed in Sheol, you are there.
If I take the wings of the morning
    and settle at the farthest limits of the sea,
even there your hand shall lead me,
    and your right hand shall hold me fast.
If I say, "Surely the darkness shall cover me,
    and the light around me become night,"
even the darkness is not dark to you;
    the night is as bright as the day,
    for darkness is as light to you.
                                    —Psalm 139:7-12

* * *

Loneliness is no respecter of age or status, but you can manage it if you will . . .

- Diagnose the cause.
- Cultivate the friend inside you.
- Find support through others.
- Do something for others.
- View life through a wide-angle lens.
- Remember **you are never alone!**

IX

HOW TO FORGIVE

Forgiving is at the heart of the Christian faith. It is the most therapeutic phenomenon the world has ever known. Nothing ever created or even dreamed about brings wholeness to life as does redeeming past wrongs. Forgiveness brings freedom from the bondage of the past. It is the catalyst for creating new and right relationships with others in the present. It is the hope for an eternal life with God.

It is not easy to forgive. Wrongs dig deep into our lives, fester, and produce pain. A child is killed by a careless hunter. A wife or husband is unfaithful. A neighbor builds a fence across another's property. A salesperson sells swampland to an unsuspecting buyer. Someone in the community creates false rumors. A friend cheats to win. It's easy to talk about forgiveness, but forgiving others is hard.

The price of forgiveness for our sin was not easy to pay. The crosses we wear and place on the altars of our churches are beautiful, but the cross on which Jesus died was an instrument of execution. Jesus' death was a beautiful giving of self, but it was brutal. His death was a painful and horrible price to pay for sin. The cross is a constant reminder of the cost of forgiveness.

Remember That All Stand in Need of Forgiveness.

Forgiving begins with a recognition of our need for forgiveness. Martin Luther had trouble accepting the goodness of his friend Philip Melanchthon. He told Philip to sin a little, because God deserves to have something to forgive. That remark couldn't be said to many of us. The need for forgiveness follows most of us daily. Mark Twain said that everyone is a moon and has a dark side which is never revealed to anyone. On seeing some criminals being taken to execution, John Bradford said, "There, but for the grace of God, goes John Bradford." Inside most of us are some uneasy stirrings about relationships that are not right or wrongs we have committed.

In the eighth chapter of John is a story of Jesus teaching near the temple. The scribes and Pharisees brought to him a woman who had been caught in the act of adultery. They placed her before him, repeated their case against her, and then reminded Jesus that the law of Moses commanded that she be stoned. "What do you say?" they asked to test him. Jesus said nothing but looked down, writing in the sand. They continued their questions. He then spoke: "Let anyone among you who is without sin be the first to throw a stone at her" (verse 7). When they heard his words, one by one they went away. Is there anyone without sin?

When we speak or think about sin, we usually consider such things as murder, robbery, and unfaithfulness. These certainly are sins, but what about jealousy, envy, excessive pride, or an uncontrollable temper? The prodigal son's sin was recognized, but the elder brother also had sin in his life. He harbored bitterness and resentment toward his brother because of the acceptance his brother received upon his return. Sin covers a wide range of activities and attitudes.

We are quick to think of sins of commission, but we sometimes forget that there are sins of neglect and omission. Jesus told a story of a man who received a talent from his master and hid it in his napkin. What did he do? He did nothing. The priest and the Levite in the parable of the good Samaritan didn't beat the man. They didn't rob him. They simply walked by. They did nothing. They passed by on the other side. Some wrongs are things that have been left undone—the opportunity we did not seize, the good we could have done, the word we did not speak.

Martin Niemöller relates a story from World War II in Germany when unjustified executions were rampant. Along with others, he was detained for questioning and probable sentencing by the Nazis. They called for all the Jews to come forward. He wasn't a Jew, so he said nothing. They called for the Communists to come forth. He wasn't one of them, so he remained silent. They called for the Catholics. He was a Protestant, so he stayed in his place. When they finally called for him, there was no one left to speak a word on his behalf.

No one is free of wrongdoing. Forgiveness is a constant need.

A few years ago the television show "Dallas" had a problem. Patrick Duffy, who played the character Bobby, wanted to leave the show, and the producers had to find a way for him to exit. They decided the best way was for Bobby to die. All the cast were present to mark the event, and that ended it—that is, until Patrick Duffy later decided he wanted back on the show. *Now* what were they to do? The writers finally came up with the idea that Bobby's death was only a dream. Everything that had happened for the entire year of his absence was washed away. After all, it was only a dream. Unlike events on a television drama, sin cannot be dreamed away. Sin can, however, be forgiven.

Louisa Fletcher's poem speaks for all of us.

> I wish that there were some wonderful place
> Called the Land of Beginning Again

Jesus came to say there is such a place. Life can begin again. Mistakes and heartaches and selfish greed can be dropped, never to be put on again.

Acknowledge and Gratefully Accept the Unmerited Mercy of God.

Forgiveness is an unmerited gift from God. Jesus told about forgiveness in the parable of the unforgiving servant. A king wished to settle an account with one of his slaves. He discovered, to his surprise, that this slave owed him ten thousand talents. This was an impossible amount of money to repay. The king ordered the slave and everything he had, even his family, to be sold. The slave pleaded with the king not to sell him and his family. He begged for mercy and promised that he would repay everything, a promise he could not possibly keep. "Out of pity for him, the lord of the slave released him and forgave him the debt" (Matthew 18:27). No strings were attached to the king's forgiveness. It was a gift.

In the same way, God forgives us. We owe so much that there is no way for us ever to repay it. What a feeling it must have been for that slave to be forgiven his debt, and what a feeling it is for us to know that God intervenes in our lives with such forgiving love. Through the suffering and death of Jesus on the cross at Calvary, we are released and set free through the mercy of the Lord. This is what Julia Johnston had in mind when she wrote these words:

> Marvelous grace of our loving Lord,
> grace that exceeds our sin and our guilt!
> Yonder on Calvary's mount outpoured,
> there where the blood of the Lamb was spilt.
> Grace, grace, God's grace,
> grace that will pardon and cleanse within;
> grace, grace, God's grace,
> grace that is greater than all our sin!

In her book *Tramp for the Lord*, Corrie Ten Boom tells about her visit to Germany after the war.

> I had come from Holland to defeated Germany with the message that God forgives. It was the truth they needed most to hear in that bitter,

bombed-out land, and I gave them my favorite mental picture. Maybe because the sea is never far from a Hollander's mind, I like to think that that's where forgiven sins are thrown. "When we confess our sins," I said, "God casts them into the deepest ocean, gone forever. . . . I believe God then places a sign out there that says, NO FISHING ALLOWED!''

I've often driven past the homeplace of Henry Clay in Lexington, Kentucky. At one time in his illustrious career, Mr. Clay fell hopelessly into debt. As the story goes, his moral principles would not allow his debts to go unpaid, so he prepared to sell his holdings. Some of his friends heard of his financial plight and went to the local bank to pay the forty thousand dollars he owed. The banker wanted to know what he could tell Mr. Clay about the payment. They suggested he tell Mr. Clay that his debt was paid by some of his friends. When Mr. Clay heard the news, it was more than he could stand. He was a tough leader, but, on that occasion, his eyes filled with tears. He asked how anyone could do that for him.

God's gift to us canceled far more than a financial debt. Frederick Faber must have been thinking of this mercy of God when he wrote these words:

> There's a wideness in God's mercy
> like the wideness of the sea;
> there's a kindness in God's justice,
> which is more than liberty.

The forgiving mercy of the Lord is almost beyond our comprehension. We did nothing to earn it. Forgiveness is freely given, but it is not forced upon us. We must accept it.

When Andrew Jackson was president of the United States, a criminal who had robbed the U. S. mail and had murdered a man was awaiting execution in prison. Jackson saw fit to write a full pardon for the man, but, for some reason, the man refused to accept it. What now? Was he pardoned or not? After long deliberation by the Supreme Court, Chief Justice John Marshall reported that the value of a pardon depends on its acceptance by the person implicated. Acknowledging that it is unlikely that one sentenced to death would refuse to accept a pardon, Marshall ruled that without acceptance, there is no pardon. The prisoner died on the gallows because he spurned the president's pardon.

A story is told about a little boy who visited the Washington Monument and noticed a guard standing beside it. He said to the guard, "I want to buy it." The guard stooped down and said, "How much money do you have?" The boy reached in his pocket and pulled out a quarter. The guard said, "That's not enough." The boy replied, "I thought you would say that." So he pulled out nine cents more. The guard looked down at the boy and said, "You need to understand three things. First, thirty-four cents is not enough. In fact, thirty-four million dollars is not enough to buy the Washington Monument. Second, the monument is not for sale. And third, if you are an American citizen, the Washington Monument already belongs to you. Accept it."

God does not force his forgiveness upon us. It is freely given in love, but it must be accepted. Our acceptance of God's forgiveness, however, does not erase the consequence of our sin. Because God's forgiveness is freely given in love, we may be tempted to think that sin is no big thing. We sin, we ask God for forgiveness, and that is the end. We often forget that the person who sinned is free but the consequence of the sin remains. Jesus said to the woman caught in adultery, "Neither do I condemn you. Go your way, and from now on do not sin again" (John 8:11). Notice that he did not tell the woman he could change the consequence of her sins.

Consequence is one of the tragedies of sin. When sin is set loose upon the world, it is gone and cannot be recovered. A father came to see me and poured out his heart. With tears streaming down his face and a soul filled with guilt, he said, "I have committed an unforgivable sin against my children. It is unforgivable because it is too late for me to do anything about it. The time has passed when I can change the course of their lives." He was right. I can throw a pebble into the lake and little ripples will begin to radiate from where the pebble plunged into the water. I may later decide that I would like to retrieve the pebble, but the ripples cannot be stopped; they will go on and on until they hit some distant shore.

A mother in Texas allegedly hired a man to take the life of a neighbor woman because the woman's daughter apparently had the best chance of winning a place on the school's cheerleading team. (The alleged murder plot was not carried out; the hired man turned her in to the police.) I saw a television interview with the accused woman. She was in tears and said she was sorry. She asked for forgiveness, but the ripples from her act spread across the lake of that community. They could not be stopped.

Forgiveness does not take away the results of sin. Like the extra chip made by the sculptor's chisel, it is done, and that one blemish cannot be undone.

Respond to God's Forgiving Mercy by Granting Forgiveness to Others.

Forgiving is a natural response for those who have received and accepted the unmerited, forgiving love of God. We forgive because we have been forgiven. Like the runner on a relay team, we pass on the baton we have received from another. Forgiving is not something we decide to do; it is a loving response.

One of the most beautiful stories of forgiveness in the Bible is about a slave named Onesimus. The story begins with Onesimus stealing some money from his master, Philemon, and skipping town. This runaway slave meets the apostle Paul and is converted to Christianity. He then becomes associated with Paul's work. Through a visitor, the whereabouts of Onesimus become public knowledge, and his escape from his master is in jeopardy. Paul then writes a letter to his Christian friend Philemon and has the letter delivered personally by Onesimus.

Paul pleads with Philemon to be merciful and to receive him back, not as a slave but as a Christian brother: "I am bold enough in Christ to command you to do your duty, yet I would rather appeal to you on the basis of love" (Philemon 8). It is an unheard of request, but Philemon forgives Onesimus and sends him back to Paul as a minister.

Onesimus became a leader in the early church and probably was responsible for gathering the letters of Paul that are in the New Testament. God's love for Philemon was passed on to Onesimus, who passed that love on to us. Only through God's love can such things happen. Nothing we do reveals the stamp of Jesus Christ upon our lives as much as forgiving others.

The love of God invading our lives does marvelous things. A story is told about a banker who had a heavy heart because a man who stole from the bank was tried and convicted. The banker could have been overjoyed, but the plight of the robber's family proved to be a heavy burden for the banker. The robber's conviction left a wife and small children without financial resources. So the banker took it upon himself to provide a job for the wife and day care for the children. Upon the man's release from prison, the banker also gave him a job. Some expressed their amazement at the banker's generosity, but he responded that Christ had given him a new lease on life and he simply was passing on that grace to another.

I have heard of a family whose son was killed by a drunken driver. The family was devastated by their loss, but they eventually realized they were the recipients of God's grace and they must express the mercy they had received. With all the Christian faith they could pull together, they forgave the man who had killed their son. They visited him in prison and later pleaded for him to be allowed to spend some time outside the prison with them. They brought him into their home and joined him in speaking to others about the horror of driving while under the influence of alcohol. They forgave him and accepted him, because they, too, had been forgiven and accepted.

Sometimes our willingness to forgive may not be accepted as

it apparently was in this situation, but forgiveness still must be offered. The initiative is with us.

I once heard a story about a man whose father was murdered. He held much hatred in his heart against his father's murderer, until he became a Christian several years later. He went to visit his father's murderer in prison, but the prisoner refused to see him. So the man left the prisoner a Bible inscribed with a message expressing his forgiveness and asking to be forgiven for the hatred he had held in his heart for so long. Only Jesus Christ could fill a heart with so much love.

Forgiveness is often given without an expressed witness of the power of God in one's life. Sometimes forgiveness simply is passed on, but the reflection of God's mercy is clearly seen in the passing.

Joe Paterno, football coach at Penn State, knows how to forgive. A few years ago his team was playing against Alabama in the Sugar Bowl. Penn State had a good chance of winning the game, but a touchdown was called back because a twelfth man was on the field. When Paterno was asked to identify the player, he refused, saying the young man simply made a mistake.

Forgiving others is a response to God's love, but it also is the condition that allows God's love to flow to us. We acknowledge this condition in the prayer the Lord taught his disciples. The Gospel of Mark speaks clearly: "Forgive, if you have anything against anyone; so that your Father in heaven may also forgive you" (11:25).

Someone once said that anyone who cannot forgive breaks the bridge over which he or she must walk. This is what happened to the slave who was forgiven by the king in the parable of the unforgiving servant. What an unhappy ending to what could have been a beautiful story. The slave for whom much had been forgiven went to another who owed him a small amount and ordered him to pay. This man fell on his knees and pleaded for mercy: "Have patience with me, and I will pay you." But his fellow slave refused. He threw the man in prison until he would pay. Others knew of this and told the king. The king was angry, went to the man, and revoked his earlier pardon. The story ends, "So my heavenly Father will also do to every one of you, if you do not forgive your brother or sister from your heart" (Matthew 18:29, 35).

Like Peter, many want to know how often we are to forgive. The expectation was three times, so Peter asked the Lord if seven times would be all right. Jesus said, "I do not say to you seven times, but seventy times seven" (Matthew 18:21-22, RSV). The New Revised Standard Version says "seventy-seven times." The number doesn't matter; Jesus was saying that we are to forgive over and over again.

Forgiveness is a continuing response to God's forgiving love, which is essential if the mercy of God is to remain alive and active in our lives. Forgiveness changes our lives. When we accept forgiveness and when we forgive others, wonderful things begin to happen.

Rejoice in the Freedom Forgiveness Brings.

Edwin Markham is known for his poetic works. What many of us may not know is that he once was so bitter he could not write. He was defrauded by friends, and his life's financial savings were lost. Retirement was near, and he was without any money. He was so possessed of hate and anger that his talent for writing dried up.

One day Markham sat at his desk trying to write, but it was no use. All he could think about was the wrong done to him. In that moment, the Holy Spirit came to him with the appeal that he must somehow handle the anger and bitterness within him. In his mind he heard a voice saying he must forgive those who had wronged him if he ever were going to write again. After much prayer, he did forgive them. According to Markham, a miracle happened: The resentment was gone, and his writing began to flow. It was then that he wrote some of his most famous lines.

He drew a circle that shut me out—
Heretic, rebel, a thing to flout.
But Love and I had the wit to win:
We drew a circle that took him in!

These lines reflect the story of the prodigal son. When he came home and found forgiveness, he was free. "Bring out a robe—the best one—and put it on him; put a ring on his finger and sandals on his feet" (Luke 15:22). Those were not the marks of a slave but of one who was free. Through his father's forgiving love, he was free. Sin is a glue that holds us in bondage, but forgiveness frees us. No longer need we be captive to our own souls.

Accept the New Love of Forgiveness.

When Martin Luther King, Jr.'s home in Atlanta was bombed, an angry group of friends gathered, vowing revenge for this dastardly act. He told them to go home and put down their weapons, explaining that violence must be met with nonviolence and hate with love. Only a person who had experienced the love and forgiving mercy of God could respond in such a way.

I heard a story about a young soldier who was going off to fight against the Japanese in World War II. After seeing him off, his father said that if his son were killed, he hoped every Japanese also were killed. It was difficult for the father to continue to live with such bitterness, however, because he was a Christian. After much inward struggle, he decided that he would not allow himself to be destroyed by hate.

Some time later, news of his son's death arrived. The life insurance money soon followed. The father decided he really did not need the money, so he donated it to missions for the

Japanese. Only Jesus Christ could replace hatred with so much love.

Welcome Liberation from the Past Through Forgiveness.

While speaking at a church in Munich after World War II, Corrie Ten Boom was approached by one of the most cruel guards she had encountered during her imprisonment at Ravensbruck. She tells about their chance meeting in *Tramp for the Lord*.

> "You mentioned Ravensbruck in your talk," he was saying. "I was a guard there. . . . But since that time . . . I have become a Christian. I know that God has forgiven me for the cruel things I did there, but I would like to hear it from your lips as well. Fraulein . . . will you forgive me?"
>
> It could not have been many seconds that he stood there—hand held out—but to me it seemed hours as I wrestled with the most difficult thing I had ever had to do.
>
> For I had to do it—I knew that. The message that God forgives has a prior condition: that we forgive those who have injured us. . . . And still I stood there with the coldness clutching my heart. . . . "Jesus, help me!" I prayed silently. "I can lift my hand. I can do that much. You supply the feeling."
>
> And so woodenly, mechanically, I thrust my hand into the one stretched out to me. And as I did, an incredible thing took place. The current started in my shoulder, raced down my arm, sprang into our joined hands. And then this healing warmth seemed to flood my whole being, bringing tears to my eyes.
>
> "I forgive you, brother!" I cried. "With all my heart."

The prodigal son also experienced God's amazing love when he came home to his father. Peter knew the liberation of forgiveness after that fateful night when he denied his Lord. We share this feeling when we seek forgiveness for past wrongs. We put the past aside and we are free to live again. Oh, the liberation from the past that comes through forgiveness!

Allow Forgiveness to Restore Broken Relationships.

I experienced a beautiful moment when I met with a daughter and father who were reunited after years of alienation. The father had abused his daughter during her early childhood. In addition to the hurt of separation, hatred had filled both their lives. They had not communicated with each other in years. The daughter's children did not know their grandfather. But through a newfound life in Jesus Christ, the daughter began seeking resolution to the estrangement.

The day finally came when the two of them were reunited. Almost a generation had passed without any relationship between them. With tears and melting love, they put aside their past and forgave each other. Forgiveness restored their broken relationship. Once again they were free to love and accept each other.

A story is told about two men who had a disagreement and did not speak to each other for years. One of the men became ill, and just before he died he called his friend and asked him to sit beside his wife at the funeral. Another friend heard of this and asked why he had made such a request. The man replied that he had realized what was really important—that we must forgive one another and move on.

* * *

Forgiveness takes the fragments of life and puts them together again. It binds up wounds and heals the sickness of broken relationships.

Forgiveness is the door that opens to a new life. This new life can be yours when you . . .

- Remember that all stand in need of forgiveness.
- Acknowledge and gratefully accept the unmerited mercy of God.
- Respond to God's forgiving mercy by granting forgiveness to others.

With this new life you will be able to . . .

- Rejoice in the freedom forgiveness brings.
- Accept the new love of forgiveness.
- Welcome liberation from the past through forgiveness.
- Allow forgiveness to restore broken relationships.

Forgiveness is never easy, but it is always possible through the empowering grace of God.

X

HOW TO PRAY

The disciples spoke for everyone when they asked of Jesus, "Lord, teach us to pray" (Luke 11:1). As far as we know, this was the only specific teaching request they ever made of Jesus. They saw him calm the waters of the sea, heal the sick, restore life to the dead, and perform many other miracles. It was the subject of prayer, however, that prompted them to ask, "Teach us." Their cry for help in this spiritual discipline has been the cry of God's people ever since.

These early followers of the Lord saw and felt the power of Jesus' prayer life. On the mountain, some of them saw him transfigured by his experience in the presence of God. Late in Jesus' life, they saw the power of his struggle in prayer over the direction for his life. They saw him withdraw from the crowd for personal times with God and return to his work refreshed and filled with power. In the four Gospels, there are fifteen specific references to Jesus' personal habits of prayer. The disciples knew that, for Jesus, there was no substitute for a meaningful time in prayer.

The apostle Paul was also a person with a deep and abiding prayer life. We normally think of Paul as an action-oriented missionary who established new churches. He was teacher for the young churches, theologian to the early Christians, and preacher to the masses. All his work, however, was empowered by prayer. His word to the Thessalonians was, "Pray without ceasing" (1 Thessalonians 5:17). From the moment of his experience with God on the road to Damascus, every step he took was guided and sealed with prayer. As he instructed the young Christians about their prayer life, he used the words *always*, *continually* and *without ceasing*. His letters are framed in prayer.

Prayer is such a vital part of our spiritual quest that it has been addressed by the major writers of the world. James Montgomery ended his poem on prayer by saying:

> O Thou by whom we come to God—
>   The Life, the Truth, the Way!
> The path of prayer Thyself has trod;
>   Lord, teach us how to pray!

Ella Wheeler Wilcox reflected on the experience of Jesus on that night in Gethsemane and wrote:

> All those who journey, soon or late,
> Must pass within the garden's gate;
> Must kneel alone in darkness there,
> And battle with some fierce despair.
> God pity those who cannot say:
> "Not mine but thine"; who only pray:
> "Let this cup pass," and cannot see
> The purpose of Gethsemane.

Alfred, Lord Tennyson, wrote: "More things are wrought by prayer than this world dreams of." Our hymnbooks are libraries calling us to be active in prayer. The writings of the ages have reflected the need for a meaningful relationship with God through prayer.

The old spiritual says, "Not my brother, not my sister, but it's me, O Lord, standing in the need of prayer." I know that I need prayer, but my brothers and sisters also need prayer. We all do. Prayer is one of the most needed and wanted experiences of life.

Evangelist Billy Sunday was preparing for an evangelistic crusade in one of the major cities of our nation. He wrote to the mayor of the city requesting a list of citizens who might have a special need of prayer. The mayor, very obligingly, sent him a copy of the city directory. Everyone needs and wants a prayer life.

Understand What Prayer Is.

Although prayer has been the subject and desire of the ages, prayer is still a fuzzy topic for many of us. We believe in prayer, but we wish we could understand it better. What is this experience that the disciples wanted the Lord to teach them? **Prayer is the expression of an inner restlessness.** Prayer is a longing, a searching, a felt need for something more than we can do for ourselves. It is a desire for contact with the eternal—something beyond ourselves. Augustine, one of the early church leaders, said, "Our hearts are restless until they find rest in thee." The psalmist defined prayer:

> As a deer longs for flowing
> streams,
> so my soul longs for you,
> O God.
> My soul thirsts for God,
> for the living God.
> —Psalm 42:1-2

This restlessness is a longing for something we need for life. As a plant reaches up for sunlight and the body hungers for nourishment, so we need what the world we live in every day cannot seem to provide. James Montgomery begins his poem "What Is Prayer" this way:

> Prayer is the soul's sincere desire
> Uttered or unexpressed;
> The motion of a hidden fire,
> That trembles in the breast.

Prayer is a relationship with God. Much that passes for prayer is nothing more than an emergency call to God—a 911 call. A crisis comes, and we cry out to God.

A third-grader came rushing into his classroom one day and told his teacher, "Two boys are outside fighting, and the one on the bottom wants to talk to you." It's easy to get the drift of that request!

When we cannot care for our needs, we instinctively seek a power beyond our own. God wants us to come to him in times of trouble. God wants us to lift up our needs, but prayer is more than just a laundry list of wants. Prayer is a *relationship* in which our whole being is focused on the eternal; it is fellowship with God that is at the heart of our desires.

Matthew Henry described our relationship with God as a boatman's hook. The hook is not meant to draw the shore to the boat but the boat to the shore. Prayer is that experience with the eternal that pulls us alongside God.

Our relationship with God implies that some of our time will be spent listening. Communication is never one-way. Just as you have something to say to God, so also God has something to say to you. Sometimes we become engaged in so many things that we never take time to discuss our work with God. We drive like mad over the countryside without considering where we are going. God tries to speak to us, but we are so preoccupied that we can't hear his voice. Listening is a vital part of any relationship—especially our relationship with God.

Our relationship with God is deepened by simply being together, knowing that the other is there. There will be times when no words are spoken. Prayer, then, is just being within reach.

I once heard a story about a pastor who was serving a church in a small town. There was a man in town who never came to church but whose name came up in many conversations. Everyone seemed to know him and talked about him often.

The pastor decided that he must meet this man. Upon asking where the man lived, a friend told the pastor that he should not make an appointment but should leave his car some distance away and walk quietly to the house unannounced. The pastor didn't understand this but did as he was told. As he came near the man's house, he heard some whistling. It wasn't any particular tune—just some whistling sounds. He then saw the man working in the backyard and stopped to watch. Everywhere the man would go, he continued whistling.

The pastor approached the man, and, after a few moments of conversation asked about the constant whistling. The man said, "That's for my wife. She's blind and becomes worried when I'm not around, but she's all right as long as she can hear me whistling."

Our relationship with God can take many forms, but the most important thing is knowing that God is near. Being aware of God's presence is what one of the early church fathers called "practicing the presence."

Prayer is the power line connecting you with the mighty forces of the eternal. Prayer is opening the door for the power of God to invade your life and the lives of others.

Several years ago Norris Dam was built in the hill country of East Tennessee. Part of its function was to provide electric power for the people of the region. Shortly after the great dynamos were operating, a night worker remarked how strange it was to be in the midst of all that power and see cabins and houses across the lake lighted with kerosene lamps. Though these people lived within the shadow of a great hydroelectric generator, they did not have its power because there were no lines linking the power station to their homes. In the same way, many people today are not linked to God's power. Their prayer lines have been neglected.

Jesus knew of this power-link with God and used it regularly. When he faced heavy responsibilities, he withdrew to a quiet place and prayed. When Martin Luther faced a busy day, he began with three hours of prayer. He said he could not bear the burden of the day without it. It has been said that the disciples prayed for ten days, preached for several hours, and then baptized all day. If all of these could not handle their needs without God's power, then how can we?

The power that comes through prayer invades and empowers your life as well as the lives of those for whom you are praying. In his book *The Seven Storey Mountain,* Thomas Merton says that the prayers of someone who loved God delivered him from the hell in which he was unknowingly confined. Likewise, in his *Confessions,* St. Augustine says that his mother's prayers saved him from a debauched and pagan life. The power of prayer is without limits.

One of the fastest-growing segments of the church today is in Korea. I preached in a church in Korea and talked with the people there about the growth of the church. I asked them, "How is it happening? What is the secret? What are you doing?" Everywhere the answer was the same: "We pray! We pray for the power of God to touch the lives of those who are living without Christ." In most churches in Korea, people gather for prayer every morning before they go to work. Most of the time the prayer sessions begin at five o'clock in the morning. It is amazing to see the church buildings filled with praying people every morning.

Prayer unlocks the powerful storehouse of God and lets it loose upon the world. Prayer is a powerful force.

Practice Prayer Regularly.

Every person develops his or her own prayer habits. Because prayer is a relationship with God, everyone does not engage in prayer alike. There are some who want to give us specific instructions—how to posture ourselves, where to go, and when to pray—but it is encouraging to know that the Bible records all kinds of prayer times and habits. Paul kneeled in prayer. Jeremiah prayed standing up. David prayed sitting down. In Gethsemane, Jesus was prostrate during his prayer time.

Hannah prayed silently. Ezekiel prayed aloud. Some prayed at the temple, and others prayed in bed; some prayed in the fields or by the sea or during a battle. Although we may not go about our prayer time in the same way, we may follow some basic guidelines for prayer.

Simply begin. An advertisement tells us to "Just do it." That is the way to learn to pray. A student asked a teacher, "How can I learn to write?" The teacher answered, "Write, write, write!" Just begin. You can no more master the experience of prayer without praying than you can learn to swim without going into the water. In the book of Proverbs, there is an interesting admonition: "The beginning of wisdom is this: Get wisdom" (4:7). The way to learn to do something is to "get at it." We learn to play the piano by putting our hands on the keyboard and beginning. We learn to farm by getting out into the fields. We learn to sing by singing. Likewise, we learn to pray by praying.

Make time for prayer. Like everything else, prayer will be pushed aside unless you make time for it. A teacher once said to a group of ministers that the devil will let you keep everything else if he can take your prayer time from you. He will let you keep your Bibles, your public worship, even your Holy Communion. He knows that if he can rob you of your prayer time, he will always hold the key to your life.

Where do you find time for prayer? It is a matter of how much value you put on it. A wise philosopher said that never spending time alone with God is the result of not loving God enough. Leslie Weatherhead, the great English preacher, made much of prayer being the last thing we do at night. His idea was that our last thoughts before sleep determine the flow of unconscious thought during sleep. Cardinal Cushing looked at prayer another way. He wrote:

> You must seek Him in the morning
> If you want Him through the day.

I don't know when your prayer time will come, but I do know that you will never develop a meaningful prayer life if you leave it to chance for some free moment. You must make time for prayer.

Quiet your mind by spending a few moments apart with God. There will be times when your prayers will be a sudden cry for God's help. This is as God wants it to be. You can bring any of your needs to God. It is helpful, however, if your prayer time is preceded by a quieting of your mind. Some things demand hard work and aggressive action, but fulfilling prayer time is not one of those things. Offer yourself to God as the clay offers itself to the potter. This is what the hymn suggests:

> Have thine own way, Lord!
> Have thine own way!
> Thou art the potter; I am the clay.
> Mold me and make me after thy will,
> while I am waiting, yielded and still.

After a hectic day, you may want to relax in the presence of God. Some spend their moments of quietness reflecting on familiar scripture passages.

> I lift my eyes to the hills—from where will my help come? My help comes from the LORD, who made heaven and earth.—Psalm 121:1-2

> Protect me, O God, for in you I take refuge. I say to the LORD, You are my LORD; I have no good apart from you.—Psalm 16:1-2

> The LORD is my shepherd, I shall not want.—Psalm 23:1

> Be still, and know that I am God.—Psalm 46:10

> The LORD is in his holy temple; let all the earth keep silence before him.—Habakkuk 2:20

It may be helpful to read some episodes from Jesus' life or selected hymns. This quiet time is much like the prelude and call to worship segments of a worship service. It is a time of getting your heart and soul in readiness for an experience with the holy.

Begin by giving praise and adoration to God. When Jesus taught the disciples to pray, he gave them—and us—a model that revealed the natural progression of prayer. He began with God: *"Our Father . . . hallowed be thy name."* Once our thoughts are centered on God, we cannot help seeing ourselves. *"Forgive us"* signals confession time. Once God has cleansed us, we offer our petitions to God for help. *"Give us this day"* naturally draws us to thoughts of others, and we include them. This is a time of intercession. Jesus concluded with commitment: *"Thine is the kingdom and the glory for ever and ever."* This prayer is more than a pattern. When we begin our thoughts with God, our prayer follows a natural progression.

In many worship services, this model—or something like it—is used to lead us to dedication and commitment to God. The service begins with praise and adoration expressed in the opening words and hymn. A time of confession follows. Then there are petitions and prayers of intercession for the needs of others and the world. The service concludes with a hymn and prayer of dedication and commitment. These segments of worship and prayer are not pieces of a puzzle thrown together but an orderly progression to the throne of God. Jesus gave us this model.

Pray expectantly. To pray without expecting anything to happen is like answering the phone with "hello" and then hanging up. When we pray, we often ramble and sputter and never come out anywhere. We don't expect God to answer.

Charles Finney, a powerful preacher of years past, was a great believer in prayer and often prayed with an impatience that smacked of irreverence. He prayed with urgency and then concluded his prayer by saying that the Lord knows he is not accustomed to being denied what he asks for in prayer. Our prayers need this kind of iron in them. When we pray, we must expect something.

A word of warning: Don't allow yourself to measure the value of your prayer time by the emotional glow that may or may not accompany the act of praying. Jesus' experience on the mount of Transfiguration was an emotional "high" for him and the disciples. I have often come from my prayer time feeling the power of God in my life, and it is a tremendous feeling. God works in more ways, however, than through the emotions. It may take time for you to feel the impact of God working through and in you. If you place a plant in the sun for fifteen minutes, you probably will not notice any difference in the plant. But if you do this regularly, you will see evidence of growth. Prayer is exposing ourselves regularly to God's spiritual forces; it makes a difference.

Believe God Answers Prayer and Pray Accordingly.

Be careful what you pray for. Years ago an evangelist came to a little mountain town in western North Carolina and set up his tent on a vacant lot. Each evening during his prayer he would say, "Lord, if we are not in the center of thy will, let this old tent come down." There was a group of boys in the community always looking for something different to do to amuse themselves. They might have let it pass if he had prayed that prayer only once. But, well, you can guess what they did. They stationed themselves at the ropes holding the tent and, with knives in their hands, they cut the ropes and let the tent fall.

It is good that God doesn't do everything we ask. We ask and ask but don't prepare for an answer. Sometimes we pray for things we could not possibly accommodate.

We pray for peace as we engage in the pursuit of power. We pray that we may be useful to the poor and downtrodden, but we have no thought of doing anything about their needs. We sing the prayer, "Take my life and let it be . . . " without believing that God might really do it.

Sometimes God may expect us to be a part of the answer. The Scriptures teach us that some things cannot be done without our cooperation. Jesus cried out over Jerusalem about their unwillingness to put their hands to the task: "Jerusalem, Jerusalem . . . How often have I desired to gather your children together as a hen gathers her brood under her wings, and you were not willing!'' (Luke 13:34).

A wealthy man prided himself in being devout and good. He prayed with his family every day, praying for all the world and especially for the older couple who lived nearby. They were poor and ill, and this man dutifully remembered them in his prayers.

One day the man's nine-year-old son said to his father, "Dad, I wish I had your money." The father asked why, and the young boy said, "If I had your money, I would answer your prayers for the old couple."

The answer to prayer requires something from both you and God. Answers are not always dropped down from heaven. You may be the one God is looking for to answer the prayers you offer.

Trust God. It is amazing what God can and will do. All God's answers are not yes, however. There are some no answers and some wait answers. So it is with any request we make. If God did everything we wanted just the way we wanted it, we would be in control of the world rather than God. The Lord knows more than any or all of us. We must trust God's judgment. Sometimes God turns on the green light, and it is time for us to move on; but there also may be a red light. Whatever you do in your prayer time, remember that God can be trusted.

Don't be startled when an answer really comes. Because we are to pray with expectancy, we should not be overcome when God breaks in upon the world and our lives with an answer. Archbishop of Canterbury William Templeton used to say that coincidents happened when he prayed and nothing happened when he didn't pray.

C. S. Lewis told about some children playing a game of "Ghost." Suddenly they heard a strange noise on the stairway, and they were frightened to death. Some of us will be just as frightened when God comes in power to answer our prayers. Don't be frightened. God does hear your prayers, and answers do come.

Seek the grace to accept God's answers. In Lloyd Douglas's book *The Big Fisherman,* a Roman officer prays for Peter's life. This is the Peter who fell asleep in the garden with Jesus and now is in Rome facing a cross of his own. Even with the officer's prayers, Peter is condemned to crucifixion. The Roman soldier tells Peter that he prayed for him but that it didn't do any good. Peter's response is that it must have done him good, because he has not been afraid.

Sometimes our sincere prayers are not answered as we might wish. Like some of the personalities of the Bible, we are troubled that God doesn't break in upon our lives and relieve us of our troubles. In those cases we need God's grace, but often we have difficulty accepting it.

At Gethsemane Jesus prayed with all his might. It was not a quiet, meditative prayer time. It was a crisis situation, because his life was in the balance. In that instant, he gave us an important example: "Not my will, but yours be done." Putting yourself within the power of God's grace will not always bring what you may want, but it will be sufficient. The last lines of the hymn "Where He Leads Me" remind us of this.

> He will give me grace and glory,
> and go with me, with me all the way.

Remember that God is always with you. The psalmist cried for all of us when he wanted to know if God had departed from him. We sometimes feel that way also, but God never leaves us. God is always at our elbow, keeping watch over everything we do.

This was the glory of the gift of the Holy Spirit. With the ascension of Jesus into heaven, the Holy Spirit was given to be a constant companion to us. Whatever you do and wherever you go, God is near. "And remember, I am with you always" (Matthew 28:20).

* * *

A pastor said he had been praying for a revival in his congregation. He shared that he had invested large amounts of time in serious prayer for his church family. After several months of diligent prayer he commented, "Since I started really praying, God apparently has not done anything for the people I have been praying for, but my . . . how God has worked me over since I really started praying."

The greatest power in the universe is awaiting your prayers. Prayer can alter the course of the world. It can bring healing to the sick. It can ignite a smoldering congregation into a brilliant fire. It can relieve the pain and hurt of a distressed and impoverished people. And it can make you an instrument of God. That is what God wants and needs today. All you have to do is . . .

- Understand what prayer is.
- Practice prayer regularly.
- Believe that God answers prayer and pray accordingly.

Tennyson was right: "More things are wrought by prayer than this world dreams of." Prayer makes a difference. Lord, teach us to pray.

XI

HOW TO SHARE YOUR FAITH

Practically nothing in the Christian religion is talked about more and practiced less than "sharing the faith." We know the words of the Scriptures: "You will be my witnesses" (Acts 1:8), and "Go into all the world and proclaim the good news to the whole creation" (Mark 16:15). We have heard countless sermons on the need for Christian witnessing, and we believe it. Sharing our faith is something we want to do, but "witnessing" has become such a gray area that we don't know how to sift through it.

When we mention faith sharing, our minds immediately picture a person in the airport or bus terminal confronting the hurrying people with strange questions or passing out scripture tracts. We think of random door-to-door visitation by strangers or unknown persons on a busy street corner waving a Bible and yelling into a microphone. We ask, "Is this witnessing? Is this what I am supposed to be doing? Can I do that?"

Many of us are uncomfortable with those kinds of religious activities. Confronting perfect strangers on the street and asking about their religious beliefs are foreign to our normal behavior. We want others to know what we have found in Christ, but we don't know how to put the pieces of the puzzle together. So we wait and wonder and then feel a tinge of guilt for neglecting this responsibility.

The Christian faith began with only a handful of believers. Most of the early followers of Christ were ordinary persons with little influence or wealth. These first Christians were not the well-known citizens of the time, but they made a great impact upon the world—without a printing press or radio or television. They didn't even have a mimeograph machine. They made their impact upon the world by sharing their faith each with another. The late D. T. Niles spoke of evangelism as one beggar telling another beggar where to find bread. This word-of-mouth method was used by the early church. It was the most effective form of communication then, and I doubt there is anything more effective today.

The difficulty of sharing our faith may be that we believe the work of evangelism is being done by large-scale evangelism programs. We see the big crusades with hundreds of people flocking to the stage, and they are impressive. In the church we also see the many organized evangelism programs that come from our denominational agencies. On television and radio there is a constant bombardment of appeals to take on the mantle of Christ. All this may lead us to believe that these are the methods for today's world.

Others may believe that evangelism should be assigned to the religious professionals. In the early days of the church, there was no such group. Evangelism had to be done by the young Christians, or it would not be done. It is different today. We employ people to do religious work.

Large-scale evangelistic efforts are a part of our day. Television and radio reach millions of people with the message of Christ. Church committees are working at this task. Religious professionals are witnessing to their faith, but the expectation of Christ is that we all will be witnesses. Evangelism cannot be delegated to others: "You will be my witnesses."

Some of our reluctance to witness may stem from a fear that

we will not be successful in our efforts. We cannot handle the thought of our witness being rejected. All our efforts will not be successful immediately, but the story told by Jesus in the eighth chapter of Luke is a good lesson for us.

Jesus told about a farmer sowing seeds. Some fell on the walking paths where they were trampled. Some fell on the rocky places where the earth was thin and would dry out quickly without providing the needed water for growth. Other seeds fell among thistles that choked out the possibility of much growth. Then there were some seeds that fell on good ground.

Some read this parable and see the many wasted seeds. Noted biblical scholar William Barclay reminds us that the object of this parable is the certainty of the harvest. Some seeds will not come up; some will never amount to anything; but some seeds will grow. All the seeds we sow will not come up, but some of them will. They will take root and grow, and the harvest will come.

The fact that many of us have not been "sowing" is apparent by a survey made by *Time* magazine a few years ago. A group of Americans ranked one hundred important events in history according to their significance. The results were amazing. First on the list was Columbus's discovery of America. Three events tied for fourteenth on the list: The discovery of X-ray, the Wright brothers' first plane flight, and the crucifixion of Jesus. The meaning of the cross apparently has not been communicated.

There is one necessary ingredient for faith sharing: You must have something to share. If there is nothing between you and God, you have nothing to tell. From the days of the early camp meetings comes the refrain: If you ain't heard nothing, if you ain't seen nothing, and if you ain't felt nothing, then you ain't got nothing.

This is not the case with you. You *have* heard something. You *have* seen the power of Christ at work in our world. You *have* felt something. You are different because the Lord is working in your life. You have something. The question remains, How do you share it with others?

Avoid the Pitfalls of Faith Sharing.

Don't brag about what God has done for you. The world does not respond to braggarts. Whatever God has done for you is a means of grace and not anything you personally have done. You may have much to rejoice about, but that is no cause for bragging.

Don't get carried away with commercial-sounding cliches and slick formulas. We are bombarded every hour of every day with well-orchestrated advertisements that are entertaining but also cold and impersonal. Such a method is not the way to tell your personal faith story. Tracts outlining two or three quick formulas for turning life around also are unhelpful. Salvation is more than a "quick fix." Genuine faith sharing requires much more than a catchy slogan or a colorful leaflet.

Don't try to overpower the individual. In a "Peanuts" cartoon Charlie Brown's little sister, Sally, told Linus she would be a good evangelist. Then she said that she convinced the kid who sits behind her at school that her religion is better than his religion. She did it by hitting him with her lunch box. What Sally didn't know is that the world will never be won for Christ by "beating" people into submission. We cannot force Christianity upon others.

Don't argue about theology or denominational issues. Theology is vital. Your faith should be built on solid ground. Denominations are valuable to the Christian faith. You should be proud of the church name you bear. These things, however, are not central to the story you have to tell.

Don't get carried away with spectacular examples. Everyone has heard and read stories about powerful and dramatic conversion experiences. We have heard about near-death recoveries and life-threatening experiences that raise the hair on our heads. Some high-powered evangelists of years past used this kind of story to convince hearers of the power of the Christ story. Although there are amazing stories to tell, this probably is not the way for you to tell your story.

Don't think that everyone must have a Christian experience exactly like the one you have had. God works in marvelous ways, and those ways are not always the same. God worked with Moses in one way and with Isaiah in another. Amos had one experience and Jeremiah, another. The calls to Peter and Matthew were different. The specific way God touches a life is not most important. Don't insist on making a carbon copy of your faith for another. Leave that to God.

Someone once criticized Dwight L. Moody for the way he witnessed to the power of the Gospel. He responded that he preferred his way to the way his critic *did not do it*. We can be sure that everyone will not always approve or fully appreciate our efforts in sharing the story, but we must tell the story the best way we can.

Practice Effective Faith-Sharing Techniques.

Be yourself. When witnessing to others, you are no different from who you are every day. You do not put on some special spiritual hat or drape yourself in some peculiar religious garb. Witnessing is an overflow of the Christian experience; it is the natural expression of your life in Jesus Christ. You do not have one voice at work or home and another voice when you share your love for the Lord. You do not presume to be something you are not. You have something that will make a difference to others, so tell your story as naturally as possible.

Be a good listener. This may come as a surprise: Listening is an important part of witnessing. The world is bombarded every day and every hour with religious messages. Religious messages on television and radio tell us what to do and how to do it. Sharing your faith, however, is not an exercise in which you do all the talking. Listening may be the door that will unlock someone's interest more than anything else. There are people all over the world who are hurting from personal problems, family problems, and employment problems. Some of these folks want to know if we really care about their hurts. They need a sympathetic ear.

One hairstyling school teaches its students how to cut and style hair and then brings in a psychologist to teach the art of *listening*. Students are taught not to initiate conversation but to be good listeners.

Being a good listener opens the door for tremendous opportunities.

Give good news, and give it positively. The late Jameson Jones was fond of telling a story about a young Englishman named Alfie. Alfie had difficulty in everything he did. In his mind he was a total failure, and he sought to take his life. As it was in everything else Alfie did, he failed. A preacher came to talk to him and asked why Alfie had tried to end his life. Alfie replied there was no good news anywhere. If there were any good news in the world, surely he would have heard it from someone.

People are hungry for some "good news." The media primarily report crises. At times, the church has been guilty of contributing to the bad news. We have complained enough for centuries of hearers. Some Christians have made a priority of speaking about sin and of painting a dreary picture of the world. Telling a child day after day how bad he or she is will not change the child for the better. Telling folks how bad they are and how bad the world is will not do anything positive for them. Some may want to be raked over the coals, but that will not help them. The world wants to know there is something good for people.

E. Stanley Jones was a prolific writer. One day he was asked why he had never written anything about the devil. He is said to have answered that if you dwell on the devil too much, the devil will get you. It made more sense to talk mainly about the Lord.

We have the best news of all for the world. It is a message of hope for all who are discouraged. It is a beacon of light for all who are stumbling in the dark. It is a message of release and relief for all who are trapped in sin. We have a beautiful story to tell.

Give your witness in first person. Tell your story from your point of view. The first letter of John supports this suggestion this way: "We declare to you . . . what we have heard, what we have seen, with our eyes; what we have looked at and touched with our hands . . . we have seen it and testify to it" (1:1-2).

A group of elderly men were sitting in the park one day discussing remedies for arthritis. It was one of those high-level medical debates. One after another told the remedy that he had heard would help. The entire group grew silent when one man said, "This worked for me." The whole world will take notice when we share our personal experience of the One who has added a new dimension to our lives.

In his book *One Man's Journey,* Robert Tuttle tells of someone who came to him terribly troubled. Dr. Tuttle said he could not tell the man to trust God, because it would not mean anything to him. What he could do was share what God had done in his own life. Nothing gets attention any better than telling another what has happened to *you.*

Several years ago I heard William Holmes Borders speak to a group of preachers. Dr. Borders was one of those unique and rare individuals who make every sermon a lively experience. He began his speech by telling us what a great privilege it was for him to have this experience of being with us. He made some remarks about the theological schools we had attended and about the biblical scholars in the room. He then stated that we were experts in theological and biblical matters and that he was not. He continued by saying that he was there to tell us what the Lord had done in his life. He said he was an expert on that subject—and we were going to listen. Listen we did!

There is a beautiful story in the ninth chapter of John's Gospel. A blind man had been healed. The Pharisees were trying to get the man to say that Jesus was a sinner and was motivated by evil forces. The man answered, "I do not know whether he is a sinner. One thing I do know, that though I was blind, now I see" (verse 25). When one speaks from personal experience, there is no argument left.

In the hymn "There Is a Balm in Gilead" are these lines:

> If you can't preach like Peter,
> if you can't pray like Paul,
> Just tell the love of Jesus,
> And say he died for all.

Tell your story. That is all it takes.

Share your faith by being a living example of Jesus Christ. You may be tempted to neglect all the other faith-sharing suggestions and declare that this will be your witness. Do not neglect the other suggestions, but remember that Christian living is a powerful witness. When the life of a Christian is recognizably different from the lives of others, there are no tricks needed to attract people.

Years ago Benjamin Franklin wanted to have street lights in the city of Philadelphia. He didn't campaign for them. He said nothing about them. He simply built a light and mounted it on a post in front of his house. Others noticed it, were impressed by it, and had one built for their homes. One after another followed the example until the entire city was lighted.

A preacher I know was telling about a man who influenced his life toward Christ. The preacher said about the man, "His theology was not intellectual at all, but his witness had behind it the power of a burning conviction. He was so saturated with Christianity that it oozed out of his body and soul. Anyone coming within a block of him was infected by his faith."

The Scriptures remind us to let our light shine. Live according to Christian values. Stand for what is right. Uphold and support what is worthy and honest. Let Christ be the rule and guide of your life. The life you live will be a powerful witness.

Undergird your sharing with prayer. Nothing can equip us for our task more than spending time in the presence of the Lord. To receive power from God, we must be purposeful when we pray.

As a first-time visitor to India, I was fascinated by the prayer wheels of the religious. The people wrote their prayers on bits of paper, tied them to small wheels attached to a spindle, and whirled them round and round, sending the prayers to heaven. Often they placed their prayer wheels in the open and allowed the wind to whirl them. In this way, their prayers constantly were being sent to heaven.

We may scoff at such practices, but our prayer lives are often just as void of purpose or direction. We "send" the same messages over and over without giving them much thought. We pray the same prayers we prayed as children. There are no tears or toil in our prayers, and thus there is no power.

Arthur Moore was a powerful evangelist whose witness was penetrating. He never took credit for the success of his work but always referred to the cadre of people who spent time in prayer, undergirding his visits and preaching. He never called on anyone or permitted others to visit without first saturating themselves in prayer, because he believed that prayer power opened the doors.

We must undergird our sharing by praying for others—for others and for ourselves. It is imperative that we have God's power within us as we go about our work. We cannot do it alone.

When the opportunity comes, invite people to Christ. Everyone in business knows the value of getting the order—making the sale. At some point, there must be an invitation to act.

A story has been told about a time when Abraham Lincoln was invited to go to a church with a friend. Later Lincoln was asked what he thought of the preacher. Lincoln commented about the preacher's stature and personality and made some general observations. His friend pressed him by asking if he liked the sermon. Lincoln said no. When asked why he did not like it, he replied that the preacher never asked them to do anything.

Another story is told about a man who bought a large insurance policy. The policy was so large that the city paper carried a story about it. The man had a friend who sold insurance, and this friend was troubled because he was not the one who had sold that large policy. He asked the man why he had not bought the policy from him instead of the other person. The man with the policy replied, "You never asked me."

Could it be that some of the friends we have known for years do not love what we love because we have never asked them? We can be natural in our visits. We can listen to the hurts of people. We can talk about the good news of Christ. We can tell our personal stories. We can live a life centered in Jesus Christ. We can undergird our efforts with prayer. But, at some point, we have to give others an opportunity to act upon all we have been saying. We must invite them to Christ. There is an oft-repeated refrain in the journals of John Wesley: "I offered them Christ." Our task is no less.

Keep Four Empowering Truths Before You.

---

1. You can make a difference to someone—if you will. I have heard a story about an old man walking along the beach. He noticed a young man who was picking up starfish washed ashore and was throwing them back into the ocean. The old man asked why he was doing this. The young man replied that the starfish would die if left to the heat of the sun. To live they must get back into the water. The old man then commented that there were many starfish scattered along the beach. It would be impossible to throw all of them back. "What difference can you make when there are so many?" the old man asked. The young man held one in his hand, looked at it, flung it back into the ocean and said, "It will make a lot of difference to this one."

The world is big and full of people, but somewhere there is one in need of your witness. For that one person you can make all the difference in the world.

2. There is an urgency about your work. Jesus declared, "The kingdom of God has come near" (Matthew 4:17b). We do not understand the full meaning of that proclamation. We know the disciples expected the Lord to return immediately in all power and might, but it didn't happen as they thought it would. Two thousand years have passed, and the kingdom still has not fully come—but this should not put us at ease. For one who declared that a thousand years are as a day, your lifetime and mine are nothing. Procrastination must not be our motto. Our work must not be postponed. The time is now.

3. Sharing the faith is an expectation Christ has of his disciples. Witnessing is not an option. There is no way we can escape this responsibility and opportunity. We cannot assign the task to others. Witnessing is part of being a follower of Jesus.

4. You are never alone. Christ will always be with you in whatever you do. When the Holy Spirit came, the indwelling presence of the Lord became available to all. He will go with you, support you, and guide you in your effort. You will *never* be alone.

* * *

In my small hometown church there was a gathering time between Sunday school and worship. I don't remember many things that went on during that time, but Sunday after Sunday the conclusion was always the same. We would stand and repeat together these words:

> Lord, lay some soul upon my heart
> And love that soul through me

As you go about this task . . .

- Avoid the pitfalls of faith sharing.
- Practice effective faith-sharing techniques.
- Keep the empowering truths before you.

This work is important. God expects it to be done, and, with God's help, we can do it!

XII

HOW TO BE AN AUTHENTIC CHRISTIAN

There is a story of a young man who was studying music under the famed Pablo Casals. The young man wanted to be a good musician and worked hard at doing everything correctly. One day he played a difficult piece for his teacher and was pleased at how well it went. He then waited for an approving word from his master teacher. Instead of praise, he heard Mr. Casals say, "You are playing the notes, but not the music."

In much that is touted as "Christian," the music is missing. Many "notes" are played in the right ways, but something is lacking. Just as there are imitation diamonds and works of art, so also there is much that is proclaimed to be Christian that does not have the stamp of Jesus Christ upon it.

For some, the Christian life is based on negatives—what they do not do. I remember one who spoke regularly and willingly about the fact that he did not play cards, did not dance, and did not "run with women." That apparently signaled to him the certainty of his religious life. We have all heard the claim "I don't drink, gamble, or cuss." There are some things Christians should not do; Jesus made that clear. There is more to authentic Christianity, however, than what one "does not do."

Others equate vital Christianity with outward religious expressions. They quote a lot of scriptures or excessively wear religious symbols or sing a lot of religious songs. The late Archbishop Temple of England was a guest in a home and was getting dressed for breakfast when he heard from the kitchen a voice lustily singing "Nearer my God, to Thee." He reflected on the piety of the woman who went about her morning chores to the strains of that noble hymn. He spoke of his appreciation to his hostess. "Oh yes," she replied, "That's the hymn I use for boiling the eggs—three verses for soft boiled and five for the hard ones." Another person refuses to use any picture postcard that does not have a religious theme. Some plaster their automobile bumpers with scriptures. Hymns are great affirmations of our faith. Knowing and using scriptures are good. Religious symbols have always been an expression of our faith. But are these the true marks of a "real" Christian?

It was their undue concern for outward expressions that caused Jesus to denounce the Pharisees and scribes. They practiced their religion with zeal, but they paraded their faith to make sure everyone knew they were followers of God. Jesus said to his disciples, "Beware of practicing your piety before others in order to be seen by them" (Matthew 6:1). Jesus expected his followers to obey the demands of the law, not as a condition of salvation but as the fruits of a transformed life.

There are yet others who appraise their Christianity by their preparation for it. Studying is important. Worship is an essential ingredient for the Christian life. Retreats, workshops, and prayer times are necessary for Christian growth. Preparation for the Christian life is not, however, synonymous with being the person God wants us to be.

I am a would-be woodworker. I don't get much time to work in my shop, but I try to stay prepared. I keep my tools oiled and the saw blades sharp and true. I have hundreds of boxes filled with interesting screws and bolts and hardware. Everything is well organized. There is only one thing missing—I never build anything. I have made adequate preparation, but that's it. This is what often happens in our Christian life: We do nothing but plan.

Right living is important. Expressing our faith through scriptures and hymns and symbols is important. Adequate preparation for Christian service is absolutely necessary. These things, however, are not the whole story.

An authentic Christian is one who fulfills God's dream for the world through Jesus Christ. The expression of that fulfillment will not be the same for everyone. God did not endow us alike and does not have the same dream for all of us. Using the gifts we have to fulfill God's dream makes us authentic.

How do we get from where we are to the place where our lives are in harmony with the purposes of God? How do we become authentic Christians?

Be Sure an Authentic Christian Life Is What You Want.

I heard a story about a construction crew that was laying a drain line as part of a new building project. While excavating, the workmen uncovered a power cable directly in the path of their work. The foreman called an electrician who was nearby wiring the new building. The electrician looked at the cable and assured the foreman that the cable was dead, and that he could go ahead and cut it out of the way. The foreman asked, "Are you sure there is no danger?" "Absolutely," was the reply. The foreman then asked, "Well, then, will you cut it for us?" The electrician hesitated a moment, and with a slight smile said, "Well, I'm not *that* sure." This is a good question for you to ask yourself: Are you *sure* this is what you want?

There is a difference in wanting something and merely wishing for it. I wish I were in better physical shape, but I don't exercise much. I plan on doing it, but that's about as far as it gets. I wish I were more disciplined in my work. I think about it. I have even written some plans for improving. I read articles and books that encourage me, but mostly I go on stumbling around. Many of us only wish for a Christian life. We talk about it. We plan on it. We may even pray about it, but that's about as far as it gets.

Wanting is the mechanism that turns a thought into an act. The dream becomes focused and thus we can begin. Procrastination is left behind and perseverance takes over. Wanting starts the engine with a built-in power. When one reaches the moment of truly wanting something, an amazing infusion takes place. Alexander Graham Bell knew about this experience. He said he could not name the power but he was sure of its existence. According to Bell, when we know what we want and we are determined not to quit, the power becomes available.

Don't confuse wishing with wanting. One is a thought and the other is a power. If you are sure that an authentic Christian life is what you want, then you are on your way.

Be Honest with Yourself.

Inward honesty is not an invitation for you to begin browbeating yourself or telling yourself how terrible you are. It is an invitation for you to look inward to see what is there. It is a matter of getting in touch with yourself. Shakespeare said it another way: "To thine own self be true."

Most businesses take an inventory. It is a time for accounting. Can you do this with your life? Can you separate your spiritual assets from your liabilities? Can you do it with honesty?

Many medical centers have magnificent imaging machines that peer inside our physical bodies. A cartoon film strip for youth features such an instrument called a Motive Machine. It does not reveal bones or tissues but the motives for which everything is done. It answers the question of "Why?" for every act. It reveals life at its deepest level with absolute honesty.

Some people do not want to face themselves with this kind of honesty. A television movie told the story of a young man who suffered from dyslexia but covered up his problem by memorizing everything. A teacher helped falsify his grades, but the scheme was discovered. Throughout his school years he had concealed the truth. He couldn't face the fact of his problem. He was playing games with himself. This is the way some people live. They know all is not well, but they can't bring themselves to face it. They know something is missing, but because no one discovers them, they go on their way. Only when the young man with the reading disorder faced the facts about his life could he get help.

The early Greek plays required few actors because each actor wore several masks. Plays have changed, but the idea of wearing masks is still around. Nathaniel Hawthorne said, "No one, for any considerable period, can wear one face to himself, and another to the multitude, without finally getting bewildered as to which may be the true." Authentic Christianity demands that one know oneself. It clears the deck for the continuing voyage.

Commit Yourself to Jesus Christ.

In the play *Gideon,* by Paddy Chayefsky, the angel of the Lord recognized that God's chosen one had rejected him. Gideon had moved from desiring to serve to wanting to be served. The angel, speaking for the Lord, says, "I meant you to love me, but you are merely curious."

Many Christians have not experienced the full joy of Christ because they have been only curious about him. They have unlocked the door of their heart but have kept the little chain fastened on the inside. The door is open but still hooked. The opening is so limited that nothing can enter. It is only when we unlock the door, unlatch the chain, and get our own foot out from behind the door that the fullness of Christ can flow freely into our lives.

Allowing the fullness of Christ to flow into our lives is not always easy. Some say it is only a step. If that is true, it is the biggest step one ever makes. The Gospel of Luke (9:57-62) reminds us what it means to follow Jesus. Someone said to Jesus, "I will follow you wherever you go." Jesus said to him, "Foxes have holes, and birds of the air have nests; but the Son of Man has nowhere to lay his head" (verse 58). Jesus invited another to follow him, but the man said, "Lord, first let me go and bury my father" (verse 59). Jesus said to him, "Let the dead bury their own dead; but as for you, go and proclaim the kingdom of God" (verse 60). There was still another who wished to follow Jesus but first wanted to say farewell to those at his home. Jesus said to him, "No one who puts a hand to the plow and looks back is fit for the kingdom of God" (verse 62). Do the demands sound easy? Being a real Christian is not easy—nor is it always safe.

A story is told of a pastor whose daughter once came to him and announced that she wanted to go to Uganda as a missionary. He told her that he would not allow her to go to such a dangerous place. After explaining that Christians are imprisoned in Uganda, he suggested that she would have no problem finding missionary work in their city. Two years later she was still resolved to go to Uganda. Although he was quite upset about her decision, he went to the airport to see her off. As he watched her plane exit the runway, he commented that he wanted her to be a respectable Christian—not a real one.

The real Christian must walk to the drumbeat of God. Henry David Thoreau was a bit different from others, and he explained his difference by saying that he was walking to the beat of a different drummer.

Have you ever been walking and heard a marching band in the distance? Your step changes to the beat of the music. I often see walkers wearing earphones attached to a radio or cassette player. I can tell what kind of music they are hearing by the pace of their steps.

Those who commit their lives to Jesus Christ walk and live in a different way. For many of us, we are no different. We live and walk like everyone else. We have the same values as the status quo. We have the same attitudes, the same habits, and the same speech. We spend our money for the same things as all the others. We walk to the drumbeat of the world, and the world can see no difference in us.

Eliza Doolittle in *My Fair Lady* didn't want to hear any more words. She cried, "Show me, show me, show me!" That is what the world is waiting to see from the followers of Jesus. The authentic Christian is uniquely different. If there is no difference, why did God give us Jesus and allow Jesus to go to the cross? We are not to be strange or weird but *different*. This difference comes from a commitment to Jesus Christ.

Live Under the Power of God's Transforming Grace.

During the Civil War, many soldiers were held captive in a Nashville, Tennessee, prison. One day a woman appeared at the gate and said she needed to see her son. She had talked to the commander, and he had agreed to release her son because planting season was nearing and she couldn't work her farm by herself. She walked into the prison and told the prisoners that she had clothes for a young man. She explained that she had pretended to have a son, and that she could free only one of them. The prisoners got together and made a choice. The young man put on the clothes and walked arm-in-arm with his "mother," remarking about the plowing to be done as he passed the guard.

This story is an analogy of what God has done for us. We are adopted as God's children and are taken to freedom. This is what the grace of God is all about. We did not deserve it, and we can never live up to it.

In Ephesians 4:7 we read that grace was given to each of us. Grace was given at God's initiative and came to us even before we knew our need for it. Grace continued as God began the process of restoring us to goodness and wholeness through Jesus Christ. This was the beginning act of salvation. This grace is the present power for our maturation in the faith; it is the abiding presence in our lives, working the wonder that God has dreamed for us.

This presence of God must be trusted. You must let God work a miracle in you. God opened the sea for Moses and provided food and water for the Hebrew children in the desert. God was the security for Joshua as he entered the promised land. God transformed a greedy tax collector into a disciple for Jesus. God gave grace to the rebellious apostle Paul. God raised Jesus from the dead. Why, then, do we ever doubt the power of God's grace in our lives? Living an authentic Christian life is not easy, but we don't have to do it on our own. God's grace is sufficient for our every need.

You are called into ministry by God. Over the years there has been a cloud of mystery surrounding the idea of this "call" of God. It is through God's grace that you are called. There is, of course, the general call to everyone—to be God's child, to belong to God, to serve God. This comes through the Sacrament of Baptism. There is also a personal call of God. God calls you by name. It may not be an audible voice, but you know it is authentic. It speaks through opportunities, through doors that open, through challenges and problems needing to be solved. It is heard through hurts that cry to be healed and through people who need to be loved. God has called you, and you are in full ministry. It is the miraculous grace of God that enables you faithfully to fulfill that calling.

Arlene Anderson has written a fable about God sowing violet seeds along the roadside to beautify the earth. As God scattered them, one little seed rolled over the curb into the paved gutter. The seed begged God not to leave it there, but God told the little seed that it was just at the spot he wanted it to be. This was the place God wanted that little seed to beautify.

The little seed continued to protest, saying it could not grow there without soil or anything to eat. God told the seed that he would nourish it. God then explained that the seed had a special assignment. The seed was to grow and offer encouragement to some people who really needed it.

The little seed then told God that it would take a miracle for it to do any good there. God replied that he had a miracle just the right size for the seed and that he had arranged for an ample supply to meet the seed's need. After some additional discussion, the seed agreed to remain in that place and asked God what it must do. God replied that it simply had to be willing to stand, grow, and bloom.

Your calling and mine is to stand and grow and bloom where God has planted us. We may not always be where we had hoped. We may not play the role we had dreamed of. Our role may appear to be insignificant, but we must trust God's purpose for us. God's grace will be sufficient. You can count on it.

* * *

If you want to be an authentic Christian . . .

- Be sure an authentic Christian life is what you want.
- Be absolutely honest with yourself.
- Commit yourself to Jesus Christ.
- Live under the power of God's transforming grace.

The world needs authentic Christians. Dare to be one. It will be the greatest decision of your life!